quanundrum

[i will be your many angled thing]

quanundrum

[i will be your many angled thing]

[EDWIN TORRES]

roof books ny

Cover, Art, Book Design by Edwin Torres

Many thanks to the editors and publications that published poems from this book, my gratitude for your patience, support and gifted eyes and ears: *Best American Experimental Poetry, Big Other, Bombay Gin, Brooklyn Rail, The Canary Islands Connection* (anthology), *The Center For Book Arts, Constellation* (Melissa McGill's installation), *The Drawing Center NYC, Explorations in Media Ecology, Filiseti Mekidesi* (Elliott Sharp's opera), *From The Inside: NYC* (anthology), *Harry's House Vol. 2* (Naropa CD), *International Poetry Review, LitHub, Live Mag!, Make, Ocean State Review, P-Queue 17, Packingtown Review, Plumwood Mountain Journal, Posit, Queenzenglish.MP3* (anthology), *The Recluse, Shanzhai Lyric, Qua* (SowndHauz CD w/Matt Harle), *Visible Binary*.

Robert Duncan's quote is taken from *The HD Book*, Willie Colón's quote is from his song, *Calle Luna Calle Sol*, translation: "in handsome (risky) neighborhoods, you do not live quietly," about certain streets in San Juan, PR.

Blessings to the many angles that have directly or indirectly guided the work in this book; Miguel Algarín, Marjorie Welish, Anne Waldman, Stephen Vitiello, Antoni Tapies, Jorge Brandon, Alice Notley, El Lissitsky, Robert Creeley, Amy Catanzano, Bob Holman, Tongo Eisen-Martin, Eileen Myles, Kazuo Ohno, Albert Ayler, Pedro Pietri, Daniel Borzutzky, Kristin Dykstra, Elæ Moss, George Quasha, Joshua Beckman, Mike Tyler, Dael Orlandersmith, Jay Wahl, Joelle Stille, Libertad Guerra, Martin Bakero, Felipe Cussen, Montenegrofisher, Lucia R, Al Filreis, Nancy Cohen, CAConrad, Alexandra Tartarsky, Paulette Myers-Rich, Rosaire Appel, Slavko Djuric, Roni Gross, Lisa Sigal, Gary Green, Rocío Cerón, Brenda Coultas, Elena Alexander, Manifold Criticism, The Poetry Project, Letras Latinas, and to the continual shift of reciprocal portals.

Thank you to James Sherry for propelling me into further excavating, to Will Alexander, Ricardo Maldonado, Stacy Szymaszek, Mónica de la Torre, for deepening the pathways, and to the bloodline coursing through these pages: Felipe, Isabel, Diana, Lourdes, Elizabeth Castagna, and Rubio Jett Castagna-Torres.

This book is made possible, in part, by the New York State Council on the Arts with the support of Governor Andrew Cuomo and the New York State Legislature.

Roof Books
are published by
Segue Foundation
300 Bowery, New York, NY 10012
seguefoundation.com

Roof Books are distributed by
Small Press Distribution
1341 Seventh Street
Berkeley, CA. 94710-1403
800-869-7553 or spdbooks.org

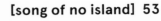

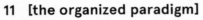

primo dawn

"to keep present and immediate a variety
of times, places, persons, and events,
in the melody we make"—Robert Duncan

"en los barrios de guapos,
no se viven tranquilos"—Willie Colón

as a start for a book of poems,
before the page is turned,
let the first quote set a stage for
the second, to point towards
the crawl at the margins, along the river
of this book, where page numbers gather
— as both ink and loop — the pull of questions
that root in lineage before quandary,
the'nundrum of language, as sum
before turn

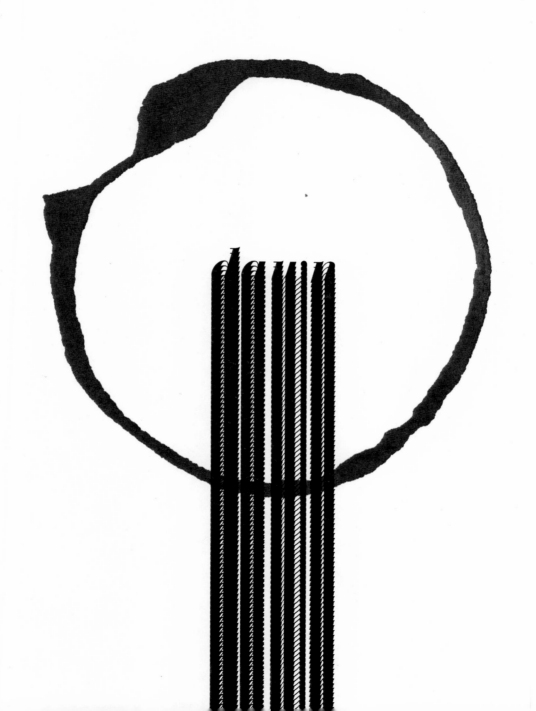

[the organized paradigm]

Imagine if you could make a film
of everything happening in the world
at the same exact time   and then you would show it all
at the same exact time at the end of the world.

Who would show it?
The sun.
Who would see it?

[tadpole at starlight]

a small infinity
has appeared on the crest of ignition
                    a curve for all things stolen
        a swipe at things that magnify

            i was infinite for a moment
traveled inside lightless eye
                    rode a width across a legion's pupil
        molded by something closer than free

            about to crash into a million years
if i could just leave the floating to smaller bugs
                    my fingers now closed my eyes hovering
        over my keys over each letter

            my frogs looking to land on soft ground
                    that's all we want, isn't it
a launchpad over stellar indications of messy instability
                            or maybe a drain to edit

            to take the universal
                    out of in
        for all things balanced
                    on lunar surf

the circumstance of delicate cognition
                    telegraphs a step — let me go up to you,
        now warm in the place i remember, and tired
— do you know how — you ask, your answer

            the one i start with

[overflow]

of one point, here, allowing … for sun
to be sun … understanding capacity
for words … here, stated by a poem's title, as *experience*

before *knowing* … of hearing the one word
alive … through the eyes of *motherfatherplanet*
to be *experience* shaped by *phase* … I should here, state

phase as *phrase* … a third knowing, always present
shaped before title, to accept more knowing than *motherfatherplanet*
will ever know … to slip, in flow

to son … who has everything he needs already
and here, in my father state … that reality, too immersive
for my everyday structure to accept

too transformative
to know, the finite composition of this body … my own
is fraught with instability

if I weren't a poet
I should here, speak … of language as capacity
of anthem as mirage

of moment as steady striation, dare I … sun's ascendant dark
in I … if the I, in the point being made
the point of capacity, overwhelming antiquity

if the I, in I … weren't a poet
I would worry that I couldn't separate existences
that there is much more of me

in the unknown ... than I will ever
need or see or be
        if I weren't a poet ... I would have imploded

        into a regular human by now
and my son ... would have left my orbit
        a long time ago

[blank dot]

it is not who we are
                as everyone
is their own we are — pulled apart
                at the core
by the we are

for the finders
finding *not*
and what *not* does
to finding
what *find* does — to *wanting*
                it is not
                — what stays
                that defines you
                — what goes
                that finds you
                is the *not* step

the one
that takes you
where the other won't
                    the one that won't
                    is not
                    the one you want
                    you want
                    the *not*
                    not
                    the *want*

i came to a wall of water
eye'd by explosion, caught
by half night — i took in the full moon
less a man than me, vision seek
by quarter noon — i took in the higher ride
shut by door drawn free — i spoke
in light-filled we, broader strokes
than me, my lower tree
climbing with me — *open a man*
                    to climb inside him
— who dared leave a seat
out on this road
along galaxy's rimshot — i took in
release, for a go at free

taken by sight
my ribbons, my eyes in flux
                    — whatever edge tells me
                            is the one i am
            it is not
            what is ours to question
            but the lesser invasion of lower limbs
            — the heated states
            of hands, of feet

... rota ... rota ... rota
... round ... round ... round
     ... inbreath
         (stay)
     ... inbreath

dot here, dot there, to again the *again*,
and there, the dot and *here*
caught one, again, to *gain* the here
to *dot* the there — and over, one more,
one other, dot to dot, to gain again its *dot*
its own *here* to be — *to open here*
i walk, between now, and there —
a call, that *arrows* my hearing,
that *falls* my here, *after* my i —
lose two letters, replace o and w, make
blank i am

              inside
              the half quarter light
a blank dot
              the full man
                     — scrape tree off sky
              sky dot

              scrape
              the seeping man —
                     i dot — here
                     dot there   — between
                                        my lower tree
                                        inside
                     the start that leaves us — sees
                     our dots that star
                            the dots we are

[celestial spine]

where the offer of walking

gave the sensory invisible

above the machinery of the visible

>where they were

>before the rivering escape

>became the encounter

among recognized forms

emboldened

the curve

>naturally alive

>detached

>*re-tached*

above our breathing

its broken faith

equal to leaving things

>before our expansive thievery

>of *we*

>with the practical split

our cognitive invisible

by the walking of the visible

in the swing of our heel

>our way to remain

>as our tail remains

>before we arrive

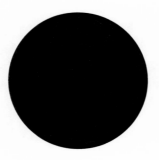

[compromise]

and they expected something bigger . . .
and they were expecting something different . . .
and they were left with parts of words . . .
and they were expected to leave with words . . .
so they left disappointed . . .
without expectation . . .

. . . so they left disappointed
. . . so they were disappointed
. . . so they left without the others
. . . when the others were left out
. . . in the way they were left
. . . they were left disappointed

and so he took out parts of words . . .
and so the parts he left in . . .
and so he took parts of what he left in . . .
and so he pointed at the others . . .
and so they expected all the others . . .
and so they pointed at the parts . . .

. . . and made the others all of them
. . . using parts that didn't disappoint him
. . . and made others be the point
. . . using parts of what he left in
. . . to be the parts that didn't point at them
. . . that didn't disappoint them

and so the parts he left in . . .
and they left in all the parts . . .
and they expected disappointing things to leave them . . .
and he stood there . . .
and he left in . . .
and he took what left him expecting . . .

. . . of what others didn't point at
. . . so they pointed
. . . while they pointed
. . . what they pointed
. . . and expected disappointment
. . . and they left him

and he expected something bigger . . .
and he took their disappointment . . .
and the parts he didn't take . . .
and they expected something bigger . . .
and you expect disappointment . . .

. . . as something bigger than it was
. . . left for someone's disappointment
. . . when the pointing was expected
. . . when you leave what you expect
and you expect
and you leave
and you point

all the parts you fit
to all the parts you make
to all the parts you want
to all the parts you take

[torn expanse]

support one star point
with vapid dismissal, *northness* in the elevated solstice
  the early *beyond* of a knowing ember
take heed, and goose across the folding migration

  many envelopes yet to fly
obelisk inscriber, affect feathernight by hopi vibrate
  cheat the clouds
arabesque the indivisible object, the seer's wall

  maybe dressed, maybe fought
might feint, all points west
  all crowns relieved by a disappeared sun
and yet here's the quiver — did you disappoint

  by disappearing — or is that clever use of d words
a dis in the prefix of evening
  a kind of darkling that takes the breath away
sleep for a day's worth of knowing

— what completes
    without —
  what is, saying
    so

    to clear the voice
inside the road — would take more
  than there is to imagine
    — more from the internal beyond

connect *look* with *how* — the breaks
  pretend to see how the puzzle of time
is a reminder, a string, a celestial wrinkle
  across how many digits left to bury

another night, a torn expanse
    blooded interweaver crossed — was it there, but look
was it us, *seeing* the look —
    the *connect* that so much of *make* — is good for

and there it goes, doesn't it —
    just something to capture, something
to remind the fingers,
    the human extension of what passes —

from one world, into the next
    the one to sit at, when stars decide to drop their glory
into the lucid *rememory*
    that passes, again, for the capture

of one more version — of removed
    interpersonal planes
        at level
    with the framing devices
            that *we* — if we can claim an *us* — can be
    the *us* we claim

for a moment of a second's impasse
    the turn — now captured
in the directionless kiss
    of mouth by brain — where the landing presents something soft

a reminder of what returns
    before the touch becomes the neck
the sift, or the eyes on the back
    where the fingers, know best the gathering
        of trails, of passages
            imagined — as hairs that stray the cerulean hollows
    — where you stroke borealis
        applauding — prima dawn

[celestial suite]: if I'm talking to you
it's because you can hear me

: : NORTHERN STAR : : :

look at how I listen
to the wrong thing again
— disturbing a sky again
            solstice calls
            for more than feel-stice
            action winter tea cup spiral
are you still with your love
who painted mine — what we say
to hear what we hear
                — *poetry can anything*
                if you let it —
wanna try to shadow twitch with tradition
look at how I listen
— to the wrong thing again

: : : EASTERN HIGHWAY : : :

            — *Sueñosima* — *when you see me* — *let me join this waking world* —
driving for how long ... and still no sun between these lines ... for how many hours on
the coast ... with Spotify numbing ... no singer's lyric ... no someone else ... no summer
sung at 4am on a lonely highway ... turn off wait by the road ... shuteye for a few winks
            — *I'm all about the luminal* —
said the liminal ... flatness is a virtue ... for a dispossessed globe ... let me close my eyes
and see if something else ... comes to me ... wants to enter ... this prime season ... of
endless white lines ... on a black year ... past horizon ... that gesture of ... *your turn now*
at the end of the poem ... our time together ... not an ending ... just a sequence

: : : WESTERN HORIZON : : :

I liked living in the not-knowing
I liked the fog I was in
when I didn't have a clue about you

there are fewer chances for mystery
as I move forward in my not-knowing
fewer moments of genuine void

that freefall is exhilarating
I wonder if that momentary arrival
in lack of ground

is made present
by the clearing
or by the letting

: : : SOUTHERN CROSS : : :

I had you in mind
the week is beginning or ending tonight
so I thought of you

the scent of your outline
mirror to mine, reach back
through a poem's longest line, made longer to prove a point

honor the lost image
the forgotten form
once fleshed in spirit

we invent realities to explain our wants
the connective tissue of missing imperfections aligned
by the failure of our falling

> *to be animal at the crossroads*
> *to pack knowingly spare*
> *to step inside the crevices by avoiding them*
> *to reciprocate knowingly spare*
> *to elevate ephemeral half-truths*
> *to gather scars of semiconscious attenuation*

if we were to scrape the burn impaled by our aim
by the faceless overture of awakening to creatures
we've never been

a crossing I visit
often, too many times, in midstride, I'm there
head turned in each direction

crescent observers
me and my crossing, both of us, wondering
who moves who

[to beget change]: to swim with the elders

if the sum of my parts, if elastic withdrawal
if lunar consistency, if relevant gash — were not mine not yours
    — *a tongue, a throat, a body*

if touch, to miss, if contact
if, your *if neck* — << *onnyerifnek* >> — not mine not yours
    — *note tongue, note throat, note body*

if the animal-ment of us, we are — is meant, we're here
    — to be

    as my heart explodes
    to be, with tree
    as my telling, ages the free — zen master
    starts a class

as quantum and erasure, digging
into the pointing of the fullness
roosting of the fullness
wrecked in company of the fullness
galavorsed by stitch of fullness
then'd by the once of full
of 'ullness
required of 'ullness
reality of 'ullness
licked of tapestry —

    — when do I stop
    repeating the selves I am
    to find the ones
    I'll be — *not mine not yours*

<< *solves iam* >>
<< *onceisle be* >>

no man I know of — no light
no color, I am
            my skin's instant color
            encounters
            a species intervention << *innerviz* >>
— *how white do you feel now* —
            says the hybrid at the march << *innerluz* >>

            how hybrid is my present
            — if the only color I see is mine

            how is your finish line these days
your lack of lightness << *ovnot-ness* >>
given privilege
            to mount privilege, over blood
            — no corpse, no hustle — there is no void
            in the telepathic aftermath

            all color is full color — *not lack of*
but all — there is no density
            in the fullness of being

            no easy out
to the escape — of *lack*
            << th*full*void >>

            there is no depth to a sheen
bouncing years off oppression
            — note melanin obsession, not mine —

in skein's einstent obsong, matter accelerates to a fulling of the instant, where the inbetween appears for the immigrant, chosen by dna to represent a lifelong quest per capita, the unconnected enclosure is a vast awaken, to use what is popular, as mechanism for survival, allowing vox among delicate overlords, due direction, ghosted complexion of raindrops on silked memory, the form of recollection, here, along the edges, errant opportunity for bravery, or syntax, you choose

*that we are
emblems on
scattered
diaphomes,
the wrested
informant,
blasted, here,
by a roadside
harrier, the
elder margin'd
by the un'er,
among class
structures, the
obeyance of
a map, sited,
as a page,
one identifies
with the mark
one makes,
the map one
makes, across
a lifetime,
scarred topos,
unspooled
as sacred,
sidestep to
the mantric
lingua, the
sudden bristle,
on back of
neck, a deeper
pulse, brought
about by the
unfamiliar, to
have fallen,
without a
push, as
expected, to
briefly fall,
without
a push*

*as my cosmos unveils
from deep in my skin — zen master says
— master say —*

 **super super — messy messy
supre'macy — supre, to see**

galactic accapellic enclosures
thievery for a stolen eclipse
solstice for the cultured Hedon Apologist —
        idolistic cantations
        reassemble our angelic intelligence

*— we, do we, to get somewhere —
— haven't you, ever got, some here,
        and wondered,
        where —*

allow us to dazzle ourselves in culture
knife the effervescent whackery
grassed in 'ullness — pointed 'ullness
what if, we — were raised to cultivate fullness
            << patina relent >>
    what if, we —
    were born intact — everything
    would have nowhere to go

    what if someone had told us
    of consciousness liberators —
we would arrive fully formed
what if all the chaos had evened out over a schism
        — we would never fall —
        << and what a short journey that would be >>

- *what is the threshold for the ravine*
- *what is distraction to the obstacle,*
  to the hand untouched, my longing for caress
- *what is the purge for dynamic size,*
  the one we are, not see
- *what is to be with earth for the flower*
- *what is the morning's ritual for the raven*
- *what is failure for the acrobat*
- *what did you receive at the center*
  of nowhere, in the middle of everywhere

Worldmatter Poet, Unvironment Sawdust
— to form mouthal relationships with your somatic daydream
invent new ways of being yourself

— what curves, on the way to touch
even under all this clothing, between teeth
and tongue, is all touch << *saltüch* >>

— what distance, for the untellable here
there is no place that sees you, born intact << *nintåk* >>

— what grieves us, for the simplest form
— a tongue, a throat, a body << *tabudî* >>

— what longs to merge, for the flower's existence
is chaos, chaos is a flower
— to the misspelling of the untellable

it is the broken that rise — unspeakably
praised by everything, to be heard in chaos
even under all this earth << *soluna* >>

the rooted structure underground, that all pages know each other, that we are embodied by each other's turn, that the movement from one of us to the next of us, is what reading does to the user, to the doer the maker, is the turn, that we are all turning, grander we, when one of us turns, here, at the spine, where the margins dare, we are more than territory for each other, islands for each other, we are selves in cell, the reading that happens, in the lived hearing, is the turn, on the guttered edge of marginal selves

to have lived the energy of earth and accept
its power, to be heard
to be partner to chaos, and not worry
of seduction
to have given in to want
in suspending absolution of the present
full of life, of 'ullness
now — if, now — sum
now — mine, remove letters
as consonants, speak *on-sonant* — speak
fully removed, each breath
syllable lack — now
evaporator of existence
now, many — now little
now to the late millennial something
as a forever

*o emerging mirror — to exact breath
on a mirror, I'm here for you
unthinged, untellable
<< myself >>*

if the world we were avoiding — was, at the final reckoning
given to us — as one, born with full toxic awakening

might we, ignite — full sensorial rebirth
into 'ullness, to accept

finally, the world we've made — as the one we partner with
might patterns << *pulse:re:pulsings* >> our pattern

so as to enter, knowingly, grand spaces — like *we*
from inside *we*, with fallen air
so as to meet << *with fullness* >>
the toes we partner with

when we say something
we are dressed
with knowing — each syllable
a world onto itself

**what did you receive
from the universe — when you saved a spider
in the middle of [blank]**
— insert city here
— insert knowing here
pattern here —

**what are the patterns to enter,
reduced — from knowing**

**difference creates desire
man — is different — than me**

I am none, that I know of —
a garment disillusioned by congregation
<< poem-muscle work your body muscle >>
I am a social afterthought

with a tongue, a throat, a body
abyss, altered, desecration — human become, of being
poet, I am, under-pre
human — among other names

I am none that I know of, still — I find
the open wound to work from
— fracture feeds my write —
in patterns of irreducible fright, engage with me, my breathing

*unselfed in
knowing
i am reduced
in knowing,
matter of flesh
as cuerpx,
of letter as
migrant rogue
among alpha,
stroke of the
immediate
palm,
marginalia
allows, where
footnote
decrees, guage
of lent culture,
note entry of
native tongue,
not nation not
island, un
island'd, state
the accepted
inclusion, for
like-minded
groovers,
among other
namers,
assembly
dictates more,
what perceives
is the animal,
not earth,
in knowing,
the patterned
un'knowing,
here, at the
feed, of reader
and margin,
th'raw undone*

th'air has
fallen, by
th'deepening
riff, th'off
ramp, density
creates no
larger human
no mycelial
bridge, divided
extrapolant,
occasional
sanskrit, here,
where eyes
divert sage,
from page to
intent, to
eco-sine wave,
man-sect, in
the middle
of nowhere,
if there were
words for
anything
resembling
message, note
how quick,
th'air diverts,
how surface is
tangle when
body shows
up, to gift
improvisation
to one, is to
note other,
dig in

there is breathing all around me
I can't escape from breathing
    I can't escape from hearing about breathing
all around me, I hear whether people can or can't breathe

the oceanic surrender of our mutual drowning

<< a surface glimmer I gargle with >>
    << a vessel in the act of tender — a body I own >>

what plagues the beginning of an envisioning
is a lack of vocabulary   — to invent imagination
         requires, nothing
             — there is no environment
        we, are environment

the world continues the world — what changes
continue, is — the world — not we
what plagues, the beginning of change
is the target not the message

<< my opening thought >>

      if the sum of my parts — were mine
    not yours — note
      being corpuscle tree
    note being

[the story of morning]

there was a man … hiding inside a boy
and then this boy … started to fly … riding high riding high in his sky
there was a sky … riding inside a man
and then this man … started to fly … follow me follow me you will fly
there was a bird … flying inside a man
and then this man … started to see … hide in me hide in me to be free
there was a tree … growing inside a seed
and then this seed … started to bleed … water me water me you will see
there was a world … rising inside a word
and then these words … came to me … talk to me

                    talk to me
                    talk to me
                    talk to me
                    talk to me
                    talk to me
                    talk to me
                    talk to me
                    talk to me
                    talk to me
                    talk to me
                    talk to me
                    talk to me
                    talk to me
                    talk to me
                    talk to me
                    talk to me
                    talk to me
                    talk to me
                    talk to me
                    talk to me
                    talk to me
                    talk to me
                    talk to me

talk to me
talk to me
talk to me
talk to me
talk to me

[quanundrum]: universe [my fast] my faster

universe got fast faster
my fast faster
universe got fast faster
my fast faster
universe got fast faster
my fast faster
universe got fast faster
my fast faster
universe got fast faster
my fast faster
universe got fast faster
my fast faster
universe got fast faster
my fast faster
universe got fast faster
my fast faster
universe got fast faster
my fast faster
universe got fast faster
my fast faster
universe got fast faster
my fast faster
universe got fast faster
my fast faster

Time represents a cycle past the moment of its creation. A desi

imagine there's a thread that runs

universe got fast faster

Writing is the same process — designing proportion among the

my fast faster

universe got fast faster

exists in that balance, a calming impetus, a kinetic interference —

my fast faster

is creation. A designed

animal dropped in mid-stream.

universe got fast faster

piece that lives beyond its moment creates new moments — at e

my fast faster

So the reader, the audience, is vital to its existing in a world alr

universe is far faster

space in proportion to

my fast faster

uage seekers among the colloquial, advertising the recipes for sta

in the act of self-swallow.

the poem approaches its consummation without a flinch.

universe got fast faster

y psyche. I imagine there's a thread that runs from that instability

portion among the lang

universe got fast faster

my fast faster

created — an animal dropped in mid-stream. The is that the work

positive space, there exists in that balance, a calming impetus, a

past the moment of its

life and is wedged in n

negative space in proportion to

igning proportion among the lan

ess — designing prop

its a cycle past the moment of its

tings in a world already

same process — designing prop

om that instability to a fascination

d piece that lives beyond its moment creates new moments — at

guage seekers, among the colloquial. Inventing the recipes for st

th apathy, with sameness, with what resonates in the steady. Whe

piece that lives beyon

e is that the work wants to be in;

my psyche. I imagine there's a thread that runs from that instabil

moment, continuously alive — by its exact not-steadiness. This i

y created — an animal dropped in mid-stream. The is that the wor

positive space, there

breath at war with their mobile premise. Where does the writer

ell-carnivore in the act of self-swallow.

fascination for how things are put together. The proportion of wh

uage seekers, among

its to be in, is what shapes the be that it becomes.

tic interference — with apathy, with sameness, with what resonat

creation. A designed

ce that lives beyond its moment

y psyche. I imagine th

e recipes for stagnant breath, at war with their mobile premise

n that instability to a fascination for how things are put together

e colloqui

rtion among the langu

is that the work wants to be in, is what shapes the be that it

ce that

created — an animal

xists in that balance, a calming impetus, a kinetic interference —

ece that lives beyond its moment creates new moments — at ev

e seeker

and is wedged in my

So the reader, the audience, is vital to its existing in a world already created — an animal dropped in mid-stream. The is that the work wants to be in is what shapes the be that it becomes.

Once you have negative space in proportion to positive space, there exists in that balance, a calming impetus, a kinetic interference — with apathy, with sameness, with what resonates past the moment of its creation. A designed piece that lives beyond its moment.

Writing is the same process — designing proportion among the language seekers, among the colloquial. Inventing the recipes for stagnant breath, at war with their mobile brethren. Where does the writer allow breath its constant removal?

A self carnivore that overtakes my life and is wedged in my psyche. Imagine there a thread that runs from that instability to a fascination for how things are put together. The proportion of what is, with what's yet to be. When proportion is introduced to possibility, the fracture ignites, so that change is born out of proportion. The process of growing, so.

This is process in action, molecular insurgents that discuss their place among the ravenous stability who threaten change with immobility.

— at every moment, continuously alive — by its exact not-steadiness.

self-swallow.

[the acrobat's last meal]

Once you are given the opening — to encounter negative space
    in proportion to positive space — a new balance is born, a calm
out of kinetic obstruction. Your gift — to become the obstruction
    — to resonate in the steady.

When proportion is introduced to combustion, the fracture ignites
    so that change is born — out of proportion. The process
of proportion and sizing it out, is the investment
    that time brings — to you, to the work.

You — are the work you interfere with
    the inherited cycle past the moment of its creation. You —
are a designed interference — beyond the continuum you design
    — the moment continuously *at moment* with itself.

Forced into your *livingness* by your exact *not-steadiness*.
    Molecular insurgents, arriving — among the ravenous stability
who threaten *change* with *immobility*.
    If — I don't move — is my move — no one moves.

Where does proportion allow breath?
    There is removal among the language seekers.
Among the colloquial — inventing recipes
    for stagnant breath, at war with their mobile brethren.

I am gored by the headline masquerading
    as *finished* — a deification of balance by demons of instability.
Approaching consumption without a flinch
    — the self-carnivore is the master of swallowing.

[to the pos-
itive moti-
vating force
within my
life]

[I spk lyric sht]

Saturday — I run
the world

Let's say this dimension > right here on this slip [underslip] would
be the misspelled in-between that engages muscle memory, my
mobile meme [I miss deep us] > for the think factories in my country
assembling what I speak [what I read a few pages from now] > let's
say our access [what it is we have to say] with [what it is we are] >
engages a few pages from now > as human [mouth].

Sunday — I'm
free

[Artment] as [party-artment] > opening [transformateur] speaks
my translation between many kinds of [my] > how can we nurture
communication with mobile i > [I-with-itidy] > the strongest
implosion we can be survives the most adaptable [-abitle] >
sub-text-re-flect [of] sur-text [ur-face] > define [what it is we see]
and [want to see] both [here] and [mouth].

Saturday — is for
the world

Sunday's — for
me

What is the misheard [appro-preux] deluxe figure formed here > of
enchanter's arousal [chatter's upanishad] and there, the superficial
afternow that speaks for me [to slit defiance] and here > in my
direction, across my blades [what speaks for me] [what would I
wear] to interword the malaprop > and there to position myself at
the edge of geo-mex-xetrics [recreating phonetically] the someone
who doesn't speak but is [mouth].

Saturday — I
change the world

Sunday — I'm
free

The under-wrong of the first hearing [or reading] is that we step
into I speak sht > knowing that before we acknowledge mistake[s]
we live them > and what if [unknowing super-glitch] there is,
mistake[s] in our everything [it is all we are] and what if [what you
saw in me] was [what you saw in you] > it is all we are to interpret
> to the matter > the mantle > the mind [it is all we are] and if it
is only in mistake[s] I am formed > let me [in my mistaken form]
be the creature I was meant to be > here > a statement, from ear to
coastal cortex [a building a people a misunderstanding] will last
longer than concrete sound > be maker, under [mouth].

Saturday — I
save the world

Sunday's — for
me

How many misheards become the reason we cross [over] each other [allowing] misdirection
> of nations to claim one misunder-nation > how glorious is it [really] to misinterpret the
deepest de-sires of misplacement > of trailing off into a certain [lift] > by allowing [flight]
a certain field > [of standing-under] how those who see [field] are the ones who belong
[enter chatter-ract-crat] > how those who live [field] are the ones who are [mouth].

Here we are [weapons of misunderstanding] unfolding familiar hearing > your meaning,
facing a direction you never meant to face > and here you are [exist] between you and
[literally] the areas you flatten > how exact to materialize excess > and here you ask [when
do you announce] your foldings as the meaning you were never intending [to own] and
here facing your own [branding] > with a name you register as [a/on/your] frame > here
you are skinny > here you are size > here [you are the one wearing you] here [the interword
enchatter enchanter] with no nation in your pocket [mouth].

Let's say the global interaction of your sht [slate] [chalice] > is in this one question [how
loved is the conviction] of the mission you announce [the clarity] of the things that shape
you] the alter [of your shape you] > the portal that inspires [so deeply] that you [need to]
shape a platform > and perform it for the world to see [can you, give yourself, maybe,
even, a page, if, that skin, be, too raw] > misspell the emotion [so we maybe, even, don't
get hurt] when we can't pronounce what it is [we're trying to] > and how vulnerable is your
misspelling > these days, in these times of [mouth].

Such molten definitions for the endearments we wield > such empathy to the listen [such
de-sire] for the tools we shape > our wrapped presentations [of the creases] we inhabit >
and right here, there is so much noise for the interweavery of selves [those sleeved
imperfections we step on] to announce our arrival [character traits we choose to broadcast]
> how we travel, by wearing threads loosened by homelands we've never endured >
through extensions we know we need > just to get through [mouth].

How everyone gone has titled your weave > with waves that bring comfort not difference
> how many far away homes [do you wear] on your mispronounciation > how tasty the
tongue of your freedom on your sht > the entered borders [you put on] the anthem
knockoffs on that frame of yours > your [isn't] nicing your [is] > the many endings you
survived with your [broken] tongue > how patterns in the color of scars are not skin but
mouth [or is it mouth that interferes] just hear me > in something I can [mouth].

the elephant is a crag that crawls in the
corner where the rooster brags a brawn
in the light, the shadow the sinister un-
derwhelped, the exotic other in search
of his next meal, in light he says of his
longing his desire for contact his holy
triumvirate a repellation against landing
against steam stenched by liquid con-
sumption, was feedback was algoritmis,
was illusino to be awakened, the ele-
phant begins a theater by painting his
face with mascurried maw, the eyeliner
pelted, the brow consumed, the strike
against wisdom a lyrical fob, he twitched
in strum the long ago moniker, he looks
at the new one, the always someone be-
fore, the always somewhere be-different,
the always something of speed, if the
energy saddled in youth were a mount,
he lumps, i would flail mambo rhapsody
ministry memed, a morning gazebo in-
habits the interruption of water, a lake-
side colored by lion and flesh, the cock
in white clothing finds a loft in soho, a
corner to call space, a gallery for goners,
we lift most high our connection with
wet, we bring heft to horror the dare to
expose, we let the blood body be body
blood brother, we bring to the line a bro-
ken wall, my mistakes left bare on a bot-

tomless floor, my recorders
resisting decay and invention,
my capture a crime against
status and quo, my accent
a war against freedom un-
posed, stanza, sonata, flora,
tone, meter, phoneme, trunk,
ankle, toe, spine, finger,
clamplight, flint, fabric, sun,
poem replaced by fire will be
floor replaced by night, we
walk out to greet you, pass
our circle, our rotation, our
equator of earthly excognito,
a center propelled by interior
dome, done in by do so, we
cross the inhabitable telling,
the seven blank story done in
by done so, by non-fat vanil-
la, what is the chain around
the foot, the one that spits up
projectile, the one on broad-
way, the in-crowd looking for
extremity, what is the base-
ist skin, the lowest unknow-
able, that brings us home,
reminder of nothing on your
surface, nothing on your lay-
er, nothing to remember of
nothing what you own

[the accent chef]

I'm needing to
understand
my specific scream
and its capacity for
size

where to locate ac-
cent by volume

the physical forma-
tion
of things I leave
behind
                      as
an interview
with the fingers

that record the in-
terview

the interview that
happens
with the acoustic
philosopher
                      at
home with the loud-
ness of fingers
                      of
things I leave be-
hind

there are specific lifetimes you form out of repetition

out of an obligation to mystery the objects we immerse ourselves in
there are specific lifetimes you form out of repetition
immerse ourselves in

particular spatialisms that confront your knowing
your knowing

as objects-formed-of-language
things you haven't seen yet

remaining where you are
below the appearances you form over a lifetime

a depth, a canvas, a paper, a body, a screen, a finger tap
a dimension of your

the objects we respaced reality

out of an obligation to mystery

particular spatialisms that confront your

as time moves through you specific importances
remaining where you are

a depth, a canvas, a paper, a body, a screen, a finger tap
below the appearances you form over a lifetime

a depth, a can

dimension a realit of your
y respaced

[cell division]

compartments
compartments of artment
come party — artment
      [*childment, woment, manment*]
      many *ins*
      going where *outs*
            won't — to emerge
            redrawn

is there enough —
            sound paint clay
            in a world
to mold my hands
            in a word I choose
            into a world — I choose to be
do I choose my world
            as my world chooses me —

— there is *noise*
and there is *'oise*
and there is also   *'se* —   all of which
          appear
          as quadrants in the mind
      — sublimity is a rhyme
          to draw to chime
          to destroy what I made

— excuse me —...*rrrrrip*...— um, I'm not —
   ...*rrrrrrack, splurk, poundddd...*
      —ok I want to watch
                  says *message* to *messenger*
                  says *stay'er* to *mover* — *immover* for some
      there was *some* building *some*
      — lots of *some*, here —
                  see, iron-forged heart
                  subtle din   of done
                              deejay splat and whook — look!
                              art matador — Artador!!! Noise-ador!!!
                  attacked by chalk'ador
                  by charcoal by string
                  by pom [*here, is your missing e — yur welcom*]

red-cheeked boy — [*I mean pom disguised as boy*]
is wandering — woundering —
      [*which means, wounding expectation with an unformed mind*]
                  as lost tape on wall —
      giftwrap the wall
                  unwrap the present
      with POW — blocks stick, don't they!
      — excuse me, RU 3D
                  in a 3D wold [*yur missing yur r — yur welcom*]
                  if only you could hear
                  the images — I hear   of air
                              landing on brush — where heart — meets skin
      [*it's that in out thing again*]
                  my world   settled
                  in my hand   on yours

look! — proto-pops! alive! on a wall! — of my own intent! —
mouthing me! — to me!
     and L.O.V.E. is a structure
     to walk on
     — a doodle a mammal — to climb on to live in
     to be L.O.V.E.
         by being — me
         out here — for world
to see   whatever shape color I be   — word, even
all   at same time —
     to live art ALIVE, noise ALIVE — am I done?

        wait, one more — FUN
          the inner crumb
I crawl through — and hum through —
        and dum dee dum through
and one more thing
        [*hummmmmmm*] — in my ear
        compartments
        — of
        hummmmmm

[nothing deletes like strange]

This is called:
Nothing Deletes Like Strange
    Mr. Entertainment was here
    …and he was boring

Esto se llama:
Nada Suprime Como Extraño
    Señor Entertainment estaba aqui
    …y él eras aburrido

This is called:
Nothing Suprime Como Extraño
    I F'booked Señor Excitement
    …and he was boring

Esto se llama:
Nothing Deletes Como Strange
    I played Pachanga con ChaCha
    …boooooring

Supre'mang me llamo:
tu sabe lo que ellos dicen
    No Jefe No FaFa
    …aburrido

This is called:
    Pontious Pilates   Mucho Macho
      Lumbago Canalgas   Nympho Mustang
    Fried Chuckie   General Tso
      Insta Pam   Taser Lefty
    Tsunami Leonard   Origami Joe

       …Knock Knock
…Who Dat
    …Jee
…Who
    …Zeus
…Wizz
    …Git!!!
…Got it
    …boooring

Hardass abuelita
Where are the Avant Garde Abuelita Poems
Quiero los poemas malditos super-chinga carrajo de cóncho cocha
cringe-inducing hardass Avant Garde Abuelita Poems!!!
    …boring

I was born with me hand up me bum
Naci de mi mano en mi culito
    …Why lookit there, it's Foreskin O'Plenty!
B.O.*…riiiing*
…Hola
dimé
…Who dis
click
    …ah-boo-rrrrriiiiii-doh

They released a private sonogram where I'm beating the crap
out of the zeitgeist — *una ultrasonografia donde golpeo la crap*
del zetigeist — ahora, tengo que suprimir a cada uno — now
I gotta delete everyone who called me
    …brrrrrrrrrrrrrrrrrrrrr

This is called:
Señor Census Dropped By
    …and he was

[occupo]

occupy / the movement
occupy / the man
occupy / the statement
occupy / the stand

occupy / the city
occupy / the missing hand
occupy / indifference
occupy / the lesser land

occupy the over
occupy the underworld

occupy / the socket
shock you-py / the occu-lord
occupy / the occulypse
a-nnoculate / 'em all

occupy / the meta-me
the enemy inside
occupy / delusion
let illusion be your ride

occupy the faith
of what you faithfully deny

occupy / allegiance
if a 'legiance / be your guide
occupy / forgiveness
if a 'giveness / let you slide

occupy / the twitter feed
the middle mobilized
occupy / the offer
of a softer genocide

occupy the populi
to get what you desire

see / the ninety nine percenter
occupy the home
see / the number one percenter
occupy the bone

see / the incomplete elitist
healin' pharacies
see / the obsolete oppression
bring you to your knees

occupy the body
modify the occupy

occupy / the tenement
the opulent / the firmament
occupy / the sacrament
the testament / the best of it

occupy / the eagle eye
the inca die / the mogrify
occupy / the elephant
the all of it / the infinite

occupy the occuli
that occupy your lord

back / to the brain to the giver
back / to the lung to the liver
back / to the blood to the river
back to the / back to the / bone

back to re-reverberation
back to ec-echolocation

back to erratic ecstatic
    tic-tectonic importation

occupy the start
the heart will occupy the i

occupy / the prayer
    occupy the ghosted tome
occupy / the gnostic
    occupy the nostro dome

occupy / the infant
    occupy fragility
occupy / the elder
    occupy ability

occupy the undecided
light you want to be

take / a dip
into matric / u la-ted / eco-mania
take / a tip
and make it trip / into / yer genitalia

lookit / what I can do
with accapella bacchanalia
lookit / what I can do
when my command is such a failure

occupy the ego
occupy humility

x-similation
x-hilaration
x-cegenation
x-hilation

x-foliation
x-calibration
x-stabilation
x-generation

occupy the higher aye to
occupy the sky

occupy / the heat wave
    let it soak your body
occupy / the street babe
    let it rock your party

occupy / the beat babe
    let it work your body
occupy / the booty shake
    make it nice 'n nawty

occupy yur yeye
occupy yur yaya yoooooooo

if i	
of i	do i
re ly	be i
on i	if i
	of why
can i	
de fy	if i
the i	de-why
of i	the i
	of i

occupy falsetto echoes
of your prophecy

occupy / la vida vida
occupado / lado malo
occupoco / loco solo
occupara / labra holler…

    agh…
        la / vida seca
    ca…
        la / sida weso
    so…
        sa / mina voco
    va…
        pa / lante sante

    end…
        collision
do we…
        end decision
do we…
        enter poison
do we…
        enter noise an'

do we…

imposit the passive
opposite the posi
tive the bit to bitter
sweet the beat to peel a

part / the body body
heart / the body body
start / the body body
break / the body…

if you SEE *you're…*
    something
SAY *you're…*
    something
SHOW *your…*
    something

    i wanna…
        feel…
        real…
        wheels…

        turn…
        one…
        turn…
        we…

occupy the rhythm
occupy the rhyme within

    this…
    is…
    my…
    time…
    to…   let
                you
                know
                it's
                not
                too
                late

occupy the feather
occupy the fate of man

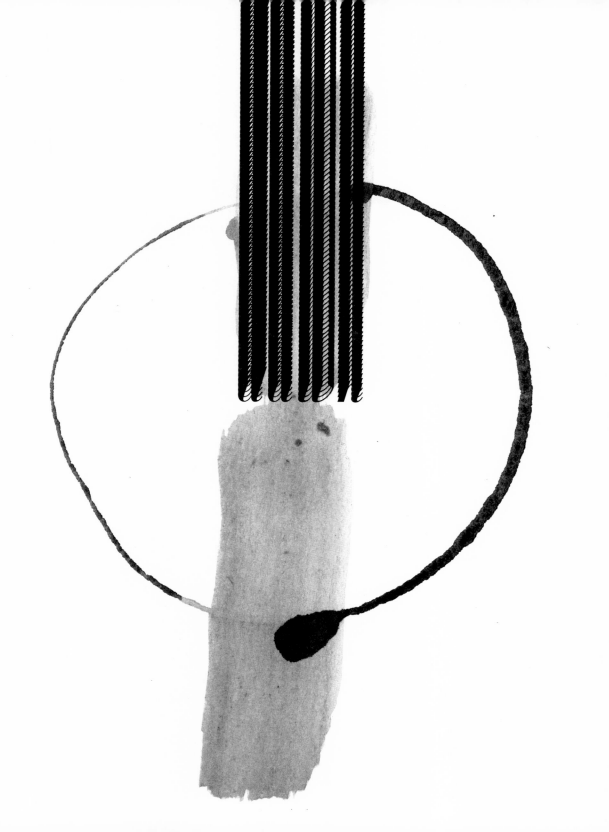

[song of no island]

from the edges that inspire me
to the edges that surround me
to the edges that define me
I'm a land of no horizon

from the galaxies below me
to the galaxies above me
to the families inside me
I'm a man of no horizon

I wanna speak American — I wanna speak my island
I wanna go where I can no — I wanna reach no island

how do you speak No'merican — how do you speak no island
I wanna know where I can go — if I can speak no island

from the waters I was born in
to the borders I will die in
to the edges I imagine
I'm a man of no horizon

as I walk the open skyway
free of all I hold inside me
what I leave for those who love me
in the land of no horizon

I wanna preach a miracle — I wanna speak no island
I wanna go where I can no — I wanna reach no island

I wanna speak American — I wanna speak my island
I wanna know if I'm alone — are you the same as I am

[immigrant earthling]

of the home — is ethnicity .
      of the city
      is home [*improvise your upbringing*]
          a galactic ethnic
          would call earth immigrant
          — of *home*
          — of *not here*

          >> dimension one — **eth** > *is*
          >> dimension two — **ni** > *not*
          >> dimension three — **city** > *home*
             is > *not* > home
             is > *not here* > home

      hallucinate your infinity
      room to room
as *we* in one huge home
are kept in one huge room
      to prevent
      roam

        << *Ah!-Ah!-Ah!—Ah!Ah!* >> [*improvise your clavé*]

of the blood — is ethnicity
      — the indigenous ethnic
      — the call of the ground
      — the reset — of new eyes, new hands
          every day
          a new line in the sand — a new dare
             >> *something pure I can own* <<

      let's stand together, shoulder to shoulder
      to see how *we* — fit in

look at the supernova pretend to be the satellite
as the galaxy in our thumbswirl
puffs and blows away >> *we are here we are here — somos otros voz otros* <<
— Immigrant Earthlings, Horsehead Nebulaes
— Quasars, Catchlings & Quantum Ricans

all that *fitting in*
controlling the *shout* — we *here* in —
animals — at home with our limbs, with letting limbs
dictate *control*

gazelles run with gazelles — avoiding obstacles without thinking
Times Square during rush hour — avoiding humans without thinking
humans can't help not think
— you can't be human alone — [ubuntu]

<< Ah!-Ah!-Ah!—Ah!Ah! >>

of the form — is ethnicity
measure your moves, by running next
to your four-legged tongue
as in — *like* likes *like*
like
human *invention* >> running the streets
like
human *intention* >> running the human
like
the pages inside my private revolution
running a world I can't see

humans are *modulation* — adept at *presentation*
>> *the day I control my language will be my downfall* <<
style is my doorway
but *edge* is my groove

of the move — is ethnicity

>> *what if I don't want to be on your team* <<

when I was in Little League
my body had yet to catch my imagination
the ball in right field and my long puppy legs
mangled any sense of balance

I tried to catch the ball, I really did
but my limbs preferred speed over physics
— I was a beautiful flop
and no one else saw that —
so the idea of *team*
was always connected
to *flop*

<u>*<< Ah!-Ah!-Ah!—Ah!Ah! >>*</u>

of the mouth — is ethnicity

>> *PASSENGERS SEATED IN THE FIRST CAR
ARE IN THE DESIGNATED QUIET CAR* <<

>> The Alter-Ricua NoRicua Project
>> an effort to save *Los Refu-gicuas*

>> those who have scampered away
>> from whatever edges they were given
>> to rediscover the ones they were born with
"show your edges, and you too can land, exactly where you are"

>> a citizen re-location program
>> where location gets *re-nationed*
>> as *translation* —
"show your papers, and you too can live, in constant tran-slay-shun"

>> a pre-dimension >> surrounding the Euclidean Barrio
>> dimension one >> **TA**, dimension two >> **Í**
>> dimension three >> **NO**
TA >> **Í** >> **NO** >> Los Indios Taíno (*loss EEN-dee-os tah-EE-no*)

"Attenxioné! Attenxioné! << RECITED THROUGH LATINX'ED MEGAPHONÉ >>
Carteros y Carta Magnas...Latinxnos...
Afrinxos, Xorixuas, Xatinxas...whateva'yu thinx of ux...
we ar' xcattered evrywhrx...no room fr everythnx...
but...take yur nombre...yu kno'...
som'thing ez to change."

>> The Alter-Ricua Refu-gicua Project
>> an effort to save the lost Boricuas
>> by *re-Rican* every *Coqui-cua* with a promise to stay
    "if I leave — I'll be right back
    don't need my flag — just want my zero
    my circular hero — my mountain — my top"

        << Ah!-Ah!-Ah!—Ah!Ah! >>

of the poet — is ethnicity
    of hybrid
    is page

    an ocean in my hand, masquerading as manifesto
    no margins in my fingers, no borders in my pen
    no ink, no stain, no endless sky

    look at the guitarist who played *salsa*
    while we waited for *grunge*
    or the foreign-American newscaster with no accent

or the newly discovered planet — obscured by light years of orbital reassignment
sneaking a peek at me, down here, trying to love the skin I'm in
just to fit in — plunge into your soft spot

with empathy *entranced* by dimension
by geography in the mangle of hybrid
— these are the lost Boricuas

the Mexican — who pretends to be Dominican —
so that his Ecuadorean visa — will get him back
to Cuba

this is about territory
and long legs
and how to step over tiny rocks
— my calling   *connection*   << PLUGIN >>
                      and *cloud*   >> PLUGOUT <<

— and maybe something about a human
who does things to be a human
— an animal in guise of animal
by owning what it's been given << *a designated human* >>

              I can >> yo puedo >> yo soy >> I be
              I want >> yo quiero >> yo soy >> I be
              I feel >> yo siento >> yo soy >> I be

the father's father holds the son's son
as the daughter's daughter holds the mother's mom
lifelines scattered across infinite bloodlines
              ethnicity has no home
              — *you can't be ethnic alone* —

                    << *Ah!-Ah!-Ah!—Ah!Ah!* >>

when I moved away from everything I knew
I didn't realize the need for difficulty
for that sense of being surrounded
by what you know you can't control

circulate with the earth
and migration will skip you by
look for new steps
and feet will betray wonder

  — *I know*
  — *I*
  — *no*

  how small
  to land
  on what you know

who owns the breath

the subject owns

owns the subject

who owns the

the matter

to transform

poetry

bodypulse

form
object

gives emotion
cuerpx
cuerpx

[i am, a am, re-am'ed, by me]

cover these waters, this body oblivious of regeneration
    of its endurable love'ness, human close'ness, surrounding close'ness
of object captured in *mouththroatheart*, lost of age, of will by age
    wished to be wish, surrendered to the not here, the not feel
that love brings after its love has loved, after object of love
    exact as love, brings its bell rung by here'ness, to tell its ancient

breathless within'ing, of its rarest input, its there'ing of breath
    in a time of water's surrounded re'render, its realest endurance of physical firm
the groundest blank once written by air, once left between finger and heft, there
    by paper by keyboard alone, to dare one, lose one
to equate earth to quake, and call that home, to call earth's destruction a poem
    shifting of skin poem, evolution of dream poem, loss of the incomplete transient poem

the wish for one more, the what you can't have at the root of the one you leave with poem
    cover the oracle day gone, cover the waking with body's impenetrable wish
to have what quakes up, before surrounding earth with you, then
    will skin its touch you, then the didn't its hopeless you
the did its arrogance, the do its implication, for how gorgeous the going calls itself home
    brings attention to the leaving, re'gorgeoused by surrounded re'renders

of bone over body, will you wish the age its walls, to capture the leaving
    that claims you, for a chance at close'ness, of human close'ness
throat of heart, did you ever close'ness the object you felt, as the one you brought
    broken the bringing of its most close doing'ness, the crammed intact
that wills you love, of ever, heart's body love, of doing, to lovable acts of doing
    as divining rod, as cover for flesh that wills, re'body flesh, re'am'ed, I am

[no yoyo]

(he's from New York) … (from Puerto Rico New York) …

(he's a new Rican) … (what they call) … (a Riqueño) …

(bein' New) … (or Trigueño) … (Speakin' New) … (or Rican) …

(a Nuyo seekin' No yorker) … (is he New) … (or a Porter) …

(a port) … (of sherry) … (Cheri Cheri) …

(Porto Puerto) … (York, oh) … (Yoko?) … (el Coco) …

(que hablas) … (se habla Coco?) … (no'Co) … (no'City) …

(port of no'City Rican) … (a Port o' Ric'er is called) …

(a bo'Ricuer) … (a Boricua) … (a boring'wha?) … (a bore) …

(this is boring) … (into my yawner) … (what chu saying) …

(what New saying) … (the new Say) … (be the new City) …

(of York) … (a yorkie) … (a pit) … (a bull) … (a toro) …

(a To'rres) … (a No'res) … (a city nono) … (a city Yorker, uncorked) …

(a boozer?) … (a bozo) … (a New bozo) … (yo soy bozo) …

(in the YO zone, si) … (yo soy the New yo) …

(that's some New yo, bro) … (yo Rican, si) … (soy No Rican) …

(he's no Rican) … (from no Ricua) … (he's no You) …

(no Yo) … (no I) … (the I) … (in I) … (is the New No) …

(I be) … (some a dat) … (New No) … (from No Ricua, bro)

[boricua in new york]

"A road is made by walking on it." — *Zhuangzi*

• • •

Dad was a dandy, all fissures and bloodline — what time does
for the poem, for the poet — aligned by *Rico-location*. Mapping
       — body to border — mover to maker — mirror to mirror to me —
       — to the father becoming the son in his dad.

Did you steal my steps — your lean *solomacho*
foreshadowing my spit-shine bravado —
in 19…what…50 — weren't we drunk on leaves before grass
by then, wasn't Whitman's Ezra, free — by then? Dad,
       how did you move when you walked these streets
       — the same ones I did on First and A?
                 Alphabet City, papi…
            what could be greater,
                 than a poet living in Alphabet City!
            I know you were a poet, papi…
                 your sister showed me your letters.
Who did you read when you got off the plane?
Your machine metal pin-stripe suit, your indigenous W2 forms
       beyond *bodega* futures — those mountainous futures
       off the grid, buried in backyard games, exhumed —
by *promesa*, by mango tree, by shade, by pen
then by 50, not 19 — would it take so much from *isla*
       to follow *lengua* before dream? Dare father, follow city
       as savior, for streets yet to be.

• • •

Swagger your *calle, Muchaco!* Swing that mandible, *Moreno!*
Capitalize your *aughts* and invade that morning stretch
       with incomplete towers, jammed up against the moon — skies
       roughed and scraped by Chrysler — a skyline envisions terror.

— what does fear do — for the poem — for the poet
— for the load at the break of my back
— for walking the talk that says more than you do? Dad,
— what am I giving you — says the son — what are you taking?
Cypher of a man
     in his 20s, in the 50s, landing —
from *Rich Port* to *Rico Puerto* — *Nueva You* to *New Yo* — know…
     what I mean — ties wide — collars ready —
cockroach corners laced — *vigor* — *vida* — *volta* — *grit* —
     ready for pearl.

• • •

    to the mover the shaker
        the doer the done — past tense, papi, rhythm tense

The giant *Do* of *ing.*
The use of *ing* — inside *Do.*
What am I *Use* of — *Do* of — *Ing* of —
What am I *ing'ing…*   here, before the moated ecliptic engines
          that surround the city of decision
          in 20…what is this…New York, my hometown
            my animal noise — anointed
            by the city who imagines the boy inside.
   Spirit's prism of the son
        carrying a throat engorged by freedom — by fingers
redrawn — by a body rewritten, as poem.

Lay the head on mountain brow
Gibralter's vow between continents — wrung
     by the call and response, of all my fathers
     their imagined savior — this poet, I…the imagined fuse — igniting
     the sublingual Father, Son and Holy Kid.

• • •

Hear — my *Chan-Chan-Chosé* — my chant of *use* — of *muse* — of *fear* —
　　Using the muse of fear — *User* claims *Doer*, on behalf of *User* — *Punto!*
　　Using the muse of fear — *Maker* maims *Doer*, on behalf of *User* — *Punto!*
　　Using the muse of fear — *Dragger* drags *User*, on behalf of *Doer* — *Punto!*
　　Infused in muses of fear — *Seer* seeks realm, at seam of sown *User* — *Punto!*
　　　　— we have *Doer*, we have *User*, now — *which you gonna be, Punto?*
　　　　— *Seer* seeks form, born of *Punto!*
　　　　— sworn by fear, galloped fear, ground in fear —
　　What is my fear?
　　　　No edge.
　　What is my edge?
　　　　No edge — followed by — no one.

My *follow* — swallowed by rebellion lung, hung at catch of throat — by *Boricua*.
　　Land of de Burgos & Brandon, coco & nut, realm inside roar,
　　Lion of Listening *User*, Caribbean pages swallowed by *Maker*
　　invented by *Taker* — tooled by *Worker* — as *Doer* before *User*.

　　Lorca left me when I left Spain.
　　Morrocco my dissident, Tetuan my city, Puerto Rico my harbor,
　　New York my home — on the back of my every trespass.

· · ·

　　　We are all islands.
　We have all traveled.
　　　We are all from somewhere else.

　　　We are all natives.
　We have all traveled.
　　　We are all from somewhere else.

　　　We are all planets.
　We have all traveled.
　　　We are all from somewhere else.

Wake of sword — worn by wake, swelled
        to *shake,* to *break,* to *choose* —
        User rues, *User* takes, *User* mights
        User blunts the borrowed maim
        the rising dwell of loin in loom.

       Mussura shames, *Musurra* storms — here...
Oza, Mezzo — Occu, Pado — Ra, Za — Man, Tra —
    — sunlit demon, traced by starfall —
        Every morning
      the world chooses
        which I to inhabit that day.

Track the sidewalks, my future rectangle, my broken angles — *the ones I follow* —
    — the margins I land in — geometric in my talk — *followed* —
    — the spoken lines I've drawn — discreet of wilder days — *followed* —
    — up to my limbs in feet — in the angle of the way the world follows me
when I leave it alone.

           • • •

      Follow the skullduggery of corpuscles
   my body as Devil Entendré —
        its never-ending construction deepens my fear
   of never leaving the ground
      down these endless streets.

Twenty-years old, when we showed up — you and I Dad —
   and how *in control* were you
      of all your limbs
  by the time you left your island dreams?
      And cities in guise of men
        — will rise from the ashes of their own discovery.
      And streets will run out on you
        — convinced of a better night.

West Side fables, Broadway songs, ancient fires — lit
by the *letting in* of all my neighbors, champion ovations — each one
                        born in movement — alive
            in the brush of their hands, their fingers passing
                    each to each — flux by flux
            followed by each — the *fingerspark* made real —
                    as all walking
                    grooms each door for its exit.

            Did we talk about the hand that holds my hand while I write?
            Let's travel *confession*
                    down *sapien* extraction — did I dare the blind arc its story?
                    Swell the tides, cursed by time —
                            keep lit the fuel, that *bodyflow.*
                            In allowing the passage of time its entry —
                    as age
                    awakens
                    to age — the hand transforms
                            — *catchermaker* — *garganta obscura.*

                            • • •

                    — *mo'tor*
                    — *throa'tor*
                    — *vo'xor*

    — increments of movement's discovery
                            awaiting infinity's incision —

    The writing; saved once by body, died once by eye, saved once
    by memory, killed by want, saved again, by want at war with itself, saved
    once by the hand that wrote it, killed in complete resurrection
    by ear, nose, skin, killed again by attacked want, dethroned
    by desire, de-tracked to remind death of its once and future
    dust, attired in possible walk, by foot, let loose of lock
    free to engage the spirit, once killed off by the heart, by fallen

beam against sunlit anointing, saved and survived, by the wreck of
its following, jeered, in the walk, from skin to mouth.

· · ·

From tongue to ear,
    what isn't complicated disappears — so, *papi*
will be around forever. The matter of talk, its own walk —
    following the *make* —
     — attached to *raza, alta pura* — to the conquests
    that define you — the alignment
   of *islas superbuenas* — you know...*nation-rubbing the accent
     off the sounds of who you know.*

What drips from these fingers, but prophesy
    born out of vertical gyre —
out of the geo-physical re-arrangement of the impossibility
    that protects us from language —
      from the search at the root of the move
    that says more than you do.

· · ·

Conductor on the D, has all the jokes: *transfer here if you're lookin' good,*
here Harlem, here Concourse, here Caldwell, CaBronX, Ocean Parkway,
Santurce, Mayaguez, the islands we jump, Coney to Puerto,
the houses we fill, *blanca* to *mami*, the families we visit
the ones we invent, first names to last, the ones
we forget, shadow to past, to speak out and actually be heard — *papi,*
trying to put to pen what might outlast him — what might unleash
his steps — what might stand up to *his* lights, right there — *my* nights.

  Crafted along *his* feet, our mutual flight — *on the streets*
  of our sons, here's to you my man, a drink —
  in neon's blinked-out declaration, lies the burning limit
  inside solitude — a city that knows

how far the poet can carry what's rooted
before losing his footing.

• • •

The cry of the Boogaloo Balseros — *Oye-me / Oye-I-E-O-U-ye*
Oye-meeeeeeeeee-ye / Oye-iye / O-uuuuuuuuuu-ye
Oye, hijo de mang-hole!
Man — Go / Hombre — Se Fue!
Maaaan-Goooo! / Hombre — Volca Me, Mang-hole, ever been called that?

Etched on family totem — *Inspiritu Espanglish* —
— severed from iron-forged heart —
a prayer for the proper man.
Decreed by life's *good* doing
to do the *correct* thing.
Taught by *strike*
to walk *straight*
to speak when *sparked* — *I was shy pops, couldn't*
answer you then, didn't know how to be wrong
and your son, at the same time.

My message lost in my
not-allowed-to-send — found in my
bottomless pen.

Did we talk about the blind beard
and facial standards for the Latin Man?
Do Young Lords
mark their turf with New Lords?
The Barrio, the Bronx —
the translucent structures that invade these pages
with the stanzas you're hearing, right now
rendered as impulse to re-take the streets?
To light the travel of phantoms
that never existed, before a flag unleashed an island.

• • •

What is the term for Puerto Rican men who don't do anything with their lives —
and I don't plan to find out.

> The body talks of sweat
> > — as engine into propulsion.

> The son says, "When will we do something?"
> When *will* we do something, what am I handing you
> what am I handing you, of strong character — and like that,
> we dig in.

> Stand tall — let *mami* see you.
> Head light — let *mami* lead you.
> Eyes from spine — let *mami* love you.
> > Her mind on miracle,
> > her silver millstone, mirror
> > to yours.

• • •

Ground to pulp, the Kickass Incompatible
> cures the bruise,
> packs the lunch,
> seams the hope — holds the Future Incompatible
> beyond the spark.
> > Soma Penetrates Corona
> > Vega-Sainted Solstice
> > Horsehead Rips Nebulae
> > Sears Blackholes Out Of Worm

> *— if you dare shoulder lineage, prepare to shoulder worm*
> > *damn straight, to earth, the world you worm from —*

Extension through delivery, digger, great as song – *Que Viva Zygoté!*
Sung alight of tongue, torn, teared in soil of song – *Que Viva Begoté!*

Ocean of sunlit integer
— of *earth* — of *son* — of *earthsontongue* —
your growing limbs
fixed on what makes you bend.
Your length — impossibly mine.
The pearls in your mouth — a temporary milestone
no tooth without fairy, no grit without grace.

Listen to your old man, my boy…let your mama lead you, did I say that already…
— my lingo full — my days of listening — replaced by ignition.
Ex Machina Nichtmagen! — Machisma Palante! — Siempre Palante!

• • •

The arc inside the journey — is where I land
out of my own way, ahead of what I made for you.
Her pointing focused
mine unmoored — take from both
your measured realm, your poet father
talking running, as if words were air.

Fall the way your knees allow, your glorious mistakes.
The way your bruises catch you, the *so much* in your baggage.
The feet you call your home, you're growing, much too fast for me —

— *When was it all right to know a world outside your own?*
— *When did you decide to include that unknowing in your play?*
— *How did all your motion make it out of what you needed?*
— *How was I the speed of such a finite land to play in?*

• • •

City is my playground, in my twenties — city swings in me
rings my bell, makes me wear newly-pressed, thrift store jackets
crisp — *I'm lookin' good* — for those who look.

Twilight determines posture, twilight
my favorite *in-between* time — between *light* and *twi*
between *yes* and *gotta go, bro.*
      I was born an *in-between* — a middle child
          a preen for subterfuge
              — solar shimmy on a din
      ChronoRicua!
           The New NoRicua —
              on time, in time…*Punto!*

              • • •

      We walk our hybrids — own our steps — each one
      the one we need.
            In my hand — is — my body
               caught by constellations
         of ancient syllables —
               drifting — in decibels I barely bruise.

      Spectre roams, atop my dome — the terror tamed by village sweets
      East Village streets and dreams that drain.

The second oldest claims the first to own the land.
Step out of comfort — something greater waits — define *greater*
define what waits, in the heat of bloodlines and one Boricua,
define sainthood and its appearance in one poet — define *poet.*

      The hand that sits atop each hand —
            each letter weighed under by its calling.
      Each landing — defined
            by the steps that follow — by a passage
               long ago determined
            by cave, by moors, by water surrounding,
               by *isla*'s invention
            by Julia, by Jorge, by Homer, by Sapien.

Homo Lupus! — Hymnal Eternal! —
Heah-luyah! — Heah-matrimos! — Moat!

And like that — we sail!

• • •

Face down, straight ahead, "I hate goodbyes," you said.
No film in your camera, the day you left — *I'm talking to you now, papi —*
       your sister, second youngest of ten,
       my favorite aunt — *she told me, papi —*
       nothing but the best for your sisters.

Did you convince yourself, your new camera, in the old country
was new technology? Using no film, for no future
       — no pictures, no mama, no cry, no smiles
       no Kodachrome goodbyes fading in your hands.

       No easy way for the second oldest
       to leave Puerto Rico, you know…just know
       when it's time — when will it be time
       — for mine to leave?

       My boy, goodbye
       — a moon, a story, a city — a sweetly dreamt of hereafter.

• • •

• • •

Dad returns, to finish what he starts —
hello the spark — he says to spark — I welcome you
to me — he says, reaching through his son.
Took a flight from home and gave it back — he says
in the form of my boy, the tall glass, the taxi generation
raised on borrowed spirits — he spills, on the ground
a drink for the bros, from his streets, to mine
to the trinity inverted — to father, son,
and solo orbit.

I return, from the gone
before entering the zone, back when these words
were a momentary fuse — stolen
from my father's edges, from guilt
for showing up, where nothing used to be.

City light has left, long ago — walking
with the sharpest shoes I got
to show the world — what I own, is not
what you think.

• • •

INSEMINATION OF THE AVANT GARDE'O'RICAN

(or) RE-INSERT-A-NATION OF 'EM AVANT GARDE'O'RICANS

(or) RE-EXAMINATION OF THE DOWNTOWN 'RICAN

> — OF THE AVANT WE-CAN
>
> — OF THE AH WANNA 'RICAN GARDE
>
> — OF THE AH WOKE UP A 'RICAN GOD
>
> — AND GOTS ME A SPEAKIN' GOD
>
> — GOTS ME HUNG UP ON A NATION
>
> — WHY ME GETS HUNG UP' YO
>
> — WHITE ME GETS HUNG YUP' YO
>
> — WIPE ME HANDS ON SOMETHIN' YO

• WHITE MAN DELUSION / HUNG UP ON SOLUTION

• GOT HUNG UP ON DELUSION / INTERNET POLLUTION

• IT'S A LITTLE BIT CON'FUSION / WRITIN' WHAT I DO 'SON

• WITH LAST NAME INTRUSION / SOME LAST NAME DILUTION

> — *MY LAST NAME'S . . . MY BLACKFACE*
>
> — *GOT BLASTED . . . ON MYSPACE*
>
> — *GOT RACE'ERASED . . . BY LIGHTNESS*
>
> — *MY WEAKNESS . . . MY LIKENESS*

• SKIN'S REVOLUTION / SIN'S EVOLUTION

• LOOKIT WHAT I DO 'SON / I'M WHITE LIKE YOU

• MELANIN ABLUTIONS / GOT MELANIN ABLUTIONS

• STARING AT THE CLUES / NO ONE KNOWS BUT YOU 'MON

• NO ONE KNOWS A HU'MON / HIDE BEHIND THE CLUES

• SIMPLIFY THE NEWS / ANOTHER WHITE MAN ON THE LOOSE

• ASSIMILATE THE BLUES / THE IMMI'GROOVE'S ON YOU 'SON

• THE IMMIGRANT IS YOU BETTER / BORDER WHAT YOU DO

• YOUR BORDER'S ON THE MOVE / BORICUAS ON THE MOVE 'SON

• BORICUAS ON THE MOON / QUE VIVA BABALOO 'SON

• QUE VIVA BABALOO

— I'M A MAN-MAN-MENTIRA . . . I'M A BAN-BAN-BANDERA

— FROM THE SLUM-SLUM-FAVELAS . . . OF MY CUM-CAM-PESIA

- **SONS OF A NATION I'M A / SEMEN OF A NATION**
- **BLOOD OBLITERATION / CHROMOSOME IMPROVE'MON**
- **DARWIN OPPORTUNE'EM / DNA THE RULE 'SON**
- **DNA THE POOL / DEMONS IN YER SCHOOL 'SON**
- **FIGHTY FIGHT THE FOOLS / BULLIES' EVOLUTION**
- **IT'S A BULLIES' EVOLUTION / NIGHT NIGHT NEWS**
- **WHITE ON WHITE ILLUSION / WHY ADMIT POLLUTION**
- **THE FUTURE LOOKS LIKE YOU / MERCURIAL CONTUSION**
- **USE'EM WORDS TO BRUISE'EM / BLACK ON BLACK AN' BLUE 'MON**

    — TRY TO MAKE YER MOVE . . . FEED A

    — DARKER PART A 'YOU . . . SEE THE MASTER

    — MASTER YOU . . . I'M A NOAH WITH NO CLUE

    — LET'EM WATERS . . . WHISTLE THROUGH

    — LET'EM WHITER WAYS . . . COME THROUGH

    — I'M A NO ONE ON THE LOOSE

- **WHAT YOU GONNA DO 'SON / BETTER MAN THAN YOU?**
- **INTERSECT THE CLUES 'SON / INTERNET THE NOOSE**
- **YER HUNG UP ON THE NEWS 'SON / HIDE BEHIND THE CUES**
- **EARTH MAN DELUSION / I CAME TO SUFFER HU'MANS**
- **I CAME TO SUFFER YOU**

    IT'S THAT GUILT THAT BUILT YA . . . GUILT WILL TRIP YA

    GUILT WILL RIP . . . WHAT YA THINK YER BUILT FOR

    GUILT WILL MILK YA . . . GUILT WILL TRICK YA

    IT'S THAT GUILT THAT BUILT . . . WHAT YA CAN'T RESIST YA

- **MIGHT MIGHT RULE**
- **BUT RIGHT WRITES RULE**
- **WHY MAN FOOL**
- **NO ONE KNOWS BUT YOU**

[my mother's brother-in-law never left the shack he was born in the world outside no match for the one inside]

let's say there's a house you pass every day
you see it as sure as I'm seeing that house right there,
I pass it every day but do I know it — his lesson starts — can I imagine
that house, what it believes in, how it frames my day
— Saul — pronounced sa-ool
blue eyes of ice fire, canyon-bronzed crevices, folded

on a sheared face, coffee mountain beard, bright notes
interspeckled philosopher raconteur — Couldabeen Poet —
he states, confirming the non-title
before I get any big ideas — don't ever go crazy because you *feel*,
don't ever feel that *loco*, is what makes you a poet, listen — he says —
there's the beginning, and there's the end

and then there's this house, my house, the one I live in,
this is a house I do know, a house I built with my hands
the sort of house, one could say, with a certain amount of logic,
that knows me in return, you see — how can an object have the same feelings
as a person of flesh and bone, that's where imagination comes in
where you can let your poetry *feel* for you — as if to affirm the awakening

he continues — you know there are songs that have real meaning
but also follow a logical path, for instance, and I only say this
because you need to understand — and here,
is where the rest of the attack surges without me, *I need to understand*
he tells me, I am semi-left alone, to balance thought
against action

as both our eyes walk over insular blinking, reminded by waterless road
that anything you touch, will touch you back, my mother's brother-in-law
ancient in his nurtured isolation, upon hearing
that he was to have an audience with a poet, *a real poet*
in his words, unleashed a lifetime of torment embroidered
by entry, his demonic shell, outside the shack he was born in

a fitting metaphor, of a house encased by a home
a world of his own making, versus a world outside, no match
for the man who believes he has dreamed his life
is the one who will choose to wake up when it's gone
the man who laughs at his first breath
will swing himself to sleep on the wings of his night

his moon, a suspension against natural intention
his landing, a forced reckoning
starved by the false never-come, he pauses
and sees an opening — the imagination is important you see, the way you can go outside
your house, the way you see what is across your street, that tree over there, for example,
do I know it sees me every day, just because I see it, how can that be, you say

how can a tree have the feelings of meat, if I chop it down for fire or to live in,
who is to say that what I live in, is not having feelings every day, the more I stay inside it
the more I wake up every morning, and see these walls, made of wood, from a tree, that feels,
who is to say that what sees me sleeping, is also not sleeping but watching me, while I sleep
the feeling of the tree I killed, is the same one that protects me from the storm,
what I killed is what loves me, you see, how can I say the same thing

about a thing that I destroyed, because it makes me warm and protected,
that's where the mind comes in, you see
if you are using your mind in your words, your words will protect you
if you destroy words — he says
with your moon, did I say, it was mind I meant, if your mind is destroyed
you know your words will protect you —

> what it is I think I want
> could be a walk along the now
> underneath the low clouds
> a skip aligned by direction
> the ground as wet as a long rest
> — let me experience belonging to a wish

[horsehead nebulae]

he sits under my legs
the shower cascading a waterfall onto his head
his tiny fingers knuckling under the catch of water drops
as if they were rain from my calves

dadah you are a waterfall
yes, I am, he crouches on the bathtub floor
my face close to the showerhead
giant over him, my eyes closed

the water wrapping my head in witness
finding its way down my back
trickling into my boy's tiny hands,
dadah I'm catching you and you are a big drop of water

yes, I am, he stretches his arms out while sitting beneath me
he holds onto each leg
you are strong dadah, as if each trunk were embedded
through the bathtub, into the ground beneath us both

hero, leader, liar
I haven't done anything to warrant a title yet
trickster, demon, pope
future and now while holding a dream

I could tell him the truth if I knew it
here in the shower-bath, the combination he loves
the ocean we pass between us
as if more than father and son were in the tub

more than pebble following shadow
as if light were in search of its holster
a constellation of infant foldings
a story in search of a seam

[of worship and flight]

why did I read about a house of snakes
if I'm trying to ease my boy's newfound fear of slithering gods
— when confronted with what can't be explained, the explanation invades
the confrontation — explaining to itself, that it's okay to spend years
on what can't be explained < *echo becoming mask* >

the unknown gathers attention from the known
when re-scrambling its own mechanism of the known < *say that again*
into your filter, your proven escape > oiled of temptation
by cover of sight — where wonder and risk meet,
is where I found the bluebird's wings

       furiously attempting to divert the black snake
       away from its nest, its home < *a valley of contradictions, here*
       before me > a bird in place of its color — a hidden nest far from danger
       where fear is waiting, to rearrange
       the brain's reception tangents, a schoolyard of saints

visitors, foreign or local, you choose — dressed in matching neckerchiefs
listening to sonic deception, imported from the Bronx, from id, from upstate New York
a fearful collection of coming outers, where to be — not-gender — is — asterisk
< *obsidian death star, in-the-closet beatheads, frostyards, cageophiles, khlebnovians,*
anti-hallmark prognosticators, devil stanza fanatics >

       the ear will pick the closest coil, to die against the weakest
       throat — there was a hero who believed
       that every curse he caught was his for everyone's failed
       blessings — the moment he knew his gift would captivate
       a million lives, is when he shifted fear to front and blue —

scared of what moves me away from what moves me < *say that again, echo*
retreats to worship > I am *fear* away from *out*, to catch the *in* — away from *in* —
the old poet reads of something of life from *this one*, of one other
from *that one*, the *out* remains — as the category of event
is its willingness to define *end* from *in*

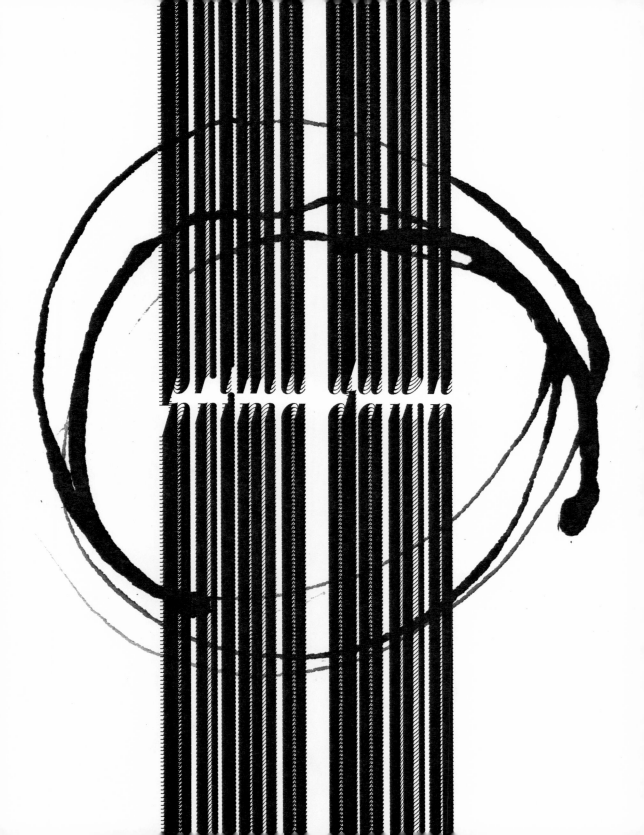

[i'm just making some noise]

group d'etat:
movement without *moment* — is not
revolution — it's just — noise

where in the mass arrest
is the alignment
of shadow's interference on solistice

does the organism contain itself
before consuming its own mass
is that where disobedience comes from
to inspire change by way of deflection
to inspire reach by way of personal god
the unreachable blog

       the further I can't touch you
       the easier I can rest
       and I'm so tired these days and that's the point

is the noise that happens by waiting
as loud as the one inside the ears
the one that unravels revolution
by gear-wrenched creed that whittles — *doing* out of *done*

the organized paradigm:
we were halfway through a conversation
in our life together and then suddenly
you disappeared
       is that *movement*
         or *noise*

       I don't need to know so much about you
       I don't want to be burdened by connection
       I do impossible very well

[bread loaves]

as you get older
your net gets smaller
weaker and bigger at the same time
your filter
          weathered, looser, finite
what gets to you now
isn't debris
but gold
          scattered nuggets
          open
          only to you
          because you're older
your level of interaction
becomes
a deeper relationship
          with the trash you leave behind
complexity
fingers
clarity
          blood from my nose
          from my pen
          feed the tiger
          to cure the bruise

[subordinate volca]

I was holding a sea creature, tightly in bed, the room was not mine, but a long dark cave with no walls, almost an ocean bottom with no water, in the dream, it was mid-dawn or dead at night, we were under covers, in my arms, yet exposed, in the dream, engaged in what might be considered aggressive cuddling, up there, on the surface, distance had become law, humanity had ascended to avoidance for survival, violence was carried out from the comfort of home, using language, crimes were committed with every sentence, isolation was no longer a mandate but a guided meditation, under the rendered open, I was released in slippage, as the shadow keeping me warm, kept floating and settling back, on whatever it was I would be one day, the creature in my arms, was cocooned in translucent shushes, hints of the binary defined our encounter, our masculine had nothing to do with our need, as if we were holding a shapeless walk, protected in a clear sack, we were viral tentacles, unlimbed by reciprocal touchlings, hovering over each other, the head was a protrusion where the neck should be, encased in hermetics, agoraphobic aurora, effable vessel, secured by Assyrian tendrils buckled on each side, with features pulled back, the face was a cross, between a pucker, and the luminescent temporal within, conundrum of the spectral, what counted for something, remained there, a clear latex funnel appeared where the mouth should be, bright red lips at the base, in my barely contained appendages, with no trace of longing, I was holding this unformed sack of flesh, while listening closely, to whispered insurrections spilling, slowly, from the inverted triangular mouth funnel, I would in turn, open my mouth over the funnel, guiding droplets of silver to engorge themselves around the cochlea, organ finding organ, we were patient, catching what bits of frenetic arousal would conjure themselves, into each other's available orifi, we remained, for years, like this, in the dream, swaying to non-existent tremors, spilling the secrets of poems, without hierarchy, or promise.

[to summon the kept immortal]

eagle of unseen origin — insistent chromature
of summoned recovery
— I'm scaling a language I don't know —
one of us, in winged invocation
is staring back, invested — in speculation
of mutual ancestry — suspended
over the cliffs
of some instant fall — it was morning
my cloudgate open — my heartshard quizzed
immortal apparition, my omniverant *not know* — rappeller
of occulate prophesy — am I to retreat the found sight
the flighted obsolescent feel
I encourage — to breathe, hovered in mid-air
a civilization's height between our species
pierced by a borrowed climb — your golden iris, my torn expanse
what we've now become — what you saw, that sun
what you gave, that mountain, what I was, that man
what I became, that flight — I re-live
your visitation, floating on heat drafts
your wings, what no ground would give — your gaze
locked in — you came to me
you saw what I would be, you waited I waited
I saw what you were, we had a conversation, it went —

say say savi savi sor sor salee saloo sweven sweven swalla swallay see on, say on, to see, to see, to see on blanking the moment, on silent integral, on obfusement, o words are coming to me, you are making me into o words, I think of you and say o words, as you imagine my grounded smote, as I imagine your wind torn slatch, I am in your o words, was that, where the o poem came from, remember the o poem, I have to find the o poem, the one about the cliffs, about adolescent menagerie, about using arm as limb, thrown to ocean, about inner quest, my early inner quest, I miss my early inner quest, did it leave, never, did it change, always, I miss that, the never leaving, what is it that I miss, that, and in, your o word offering, is where I am falling now, in your o words, offering is where I drill into sinew, my o word ommorrow, my o marrow, my ongue, my orso, my or, so, in your o word or, is my own, o, my o, in the that, of our mutual offerings, we stayed frozen like that, for hours, on that cliff, though, it felt like seconds, or do minutes feel like seconds when we, move out of the way, o of the way, do we feel like time, when given a chance for movement, do we give our solace its vertigo, when staring into eyes we can't see, yours, there in hovered magnitude, mine, there in softed o pression, of scented imperfections that form this o body, the scented immaterial of my hover you, the amount of space I claim, on a ground I call over, to call the ground I claim as the ground I'm over, o word sentient, o word logum, o word rib, o skeletal, osiris, okhemba, ojun, olorun, to inform my landing of promise, to escalate equanimity by using that word, to imply justice, by using that word, to re-train forgiveness, by using that word, to enter matter by matter's color, to enter marrow by marrow's color, to ignote color, to in color, to note color into speech, by using that word, o word ontological, I gave you one moment, a lifetime ago, a stanza ago, I gave you one word, to interpret as your own, I gave you my word, as your own, you never took, you never gave, we just stayed, cell to cell, eye to eye, intra-spectral atmospheric, it was me that stayed, in that momentary void, you were floating, what did you see, it was me that chose, my momentary sunlit apogee, my inner climb, those early days of not, how they formed what I became, how I knew to leave something, when I got too close, how that protection defined my fear, it was me that feared getting too close, how I defined my word, as yours, o word, speculation was a sentient, my body was intact, when we were younger we'd speed through, it was so much to take in, when I was older we slowed down, it was too much to take in, knowing, that standing differently, is what we've become

[i offer handling for additional belief]

let me hit return and shift
            before I start to realize, how — yet again
I throw, into think — everything but, the spin again —
                before the engine revs *again* again —

how *all* this is —
            if a sun falls, before a sky claims it
is there someone to hear it
            before it lands — is there enough to remind me
                how to hit *return*, with me in the slip
                        rightfully awoken — air out the cob webs
the incessant buzz in my mainframe
                (note laptop analogy, lets me avoid conflict)

and I love you
            in your incomplete splendor
the way your fingers tap — with missed perfection
                    I was supposed to be capturing a child's flight
            but my net has spots
                    that let in sleep, or so I remember

quiver this phase
the mention of *this* — in a *that* poem
            who said perfection
was the only web

[servile]

— who knows it all
— who thinks
they assign role-play to convenient origins
— who is my bargain
      for poetry things to happen in
— what mouth do I wear
      for a go at free

the reach that grows
when you think
you know what you want
— *is a test*   the pressure to pull back
          at the slightest drop
— *is a dare*

— blood moon
leveled against aspiration
— solved moon
the embedded chromosome
      — the thing I skip
      to hold what I need today

— who keeps order
by probing what was left — now
dare   what you want back
        to come back
    where *no way*
    invades
      yes way

[to beget the listening parade]:
what is it to move during these times

I am staying away — from the thing I don't understand
against my learned nature
      I am turning away — from the thing I know most
the thing that might fear me
      arid dispelled damnation
I am most away — from the thing I am least
      wordplay at full intention

                to move as a human — moving through movement
          to move as a hu-
             man — moving through movement
          to human as move-
             ment — to human a move
          to human as movement — to human a move

          — ***is there a responsibility here*** —

what was it about losing distance that gave us
more time to see what we were — without us —
getting in the way

what is it about interruption that questions closure
or is interruption isolation — disguised
as perception — the fear you see, the one you consume

a neural reality that knows to arrive
      — before we do — ***and now, the measure of something familiar***
inserted here, in this writing, to give us — both, me the writer
and you the reader — something to count on, to hold onto
during times of upheaval

— let me mention something of life here
                something of our movable uncertainties
— how reflection is a force
                aware of its blinding ability for *shift*
— how to frame questions of seeing
                to cope with the unsayable, the rendered inertia
— at our fingertips, of positivity recharged
                what are the heightened states of reality
— that we push past reality
                what are the morphed abilities of access
— during times of unstoppable change

                orifice orphic
I came to you, when I was at my readiest
                oracle emblem
I listened, as you split your shin

the world has grown quieter — fewer seismic
travelers, fewer machines — you can hear earth
                moving when you don't respond
                — *if I stay quiet, I won't get hurt* —

                isolation knows before we do
when it's time to leave
                — I was just now
                getting used to my breathing
before the first sound of bird
                there, in the wind, in the tree
in the passing car — far away
                but not so far, that I lose sight — of its grip
— of its wish, to see — that I'm still here, far away

loudest aeration of feather
totem for sacrum — was I deep enough
to find your cuts —
to pour, directly penumbra'd,
the obsidian refuge

what is it about a surface
approaching its center — how
we don't want to know what you're thinking
but ask *how are you* anyway — how we absorb
the usual hum of public life, at the edge of noise

less rumbling at the surface,
the virtues of vibration — distant walking, tea leaf breaking
the ramped-up volume we enter
— the understanding of a soft world
brought to surface — acoustic bird

sings free, the squeak of actually hearing, the beak
against the sun — the quietest entry
that creatures have ever had
is here, nature — taking a breath

and now, something
of joy and division — as sadness
parades noise
for the twitterati : : :

if everyone knows I am watching, if everyone hears me today
will everyone be there tomorrow, did everyone leave me today

this morning I walked in my shadow, last night I surrendered my scream
tomorrow I water my hollow, I'm telling you things you don't need

— in isolation — every sensation — gets elevation — in isolation

if gratitude is a contagion, a sign of the catchable rise
a question of human erosion, a quiver inside a demise

to see the eclipsed intervention, what humans the human we see
to enter the size we embody, to follow the follow we feed

— in isolation — I found a nation — in hibernation — I found creation

if bodies are made of existence, we're doing the best that we can
if language is made of resistance, to offer a hand for a hand

to learn what we can from our body, to honor the teachable plan
to enter the question of body, to answer the best that we can

— visit me
in my equanimity chamber
— where my bid
approaches yours

what is it about shutting down a language
portrayed by speed — that follows the call
of a shared speed

to move as a structure
                    defining mobility — to socialize reality
        by defining reality
                            << I was never that far from reality
                I was only inside my reality >>

        defining a movement — that insists
    on movement — as a structure
                    for reality — is a body map for cell division

if there was a moment to talk about flattening it was when it left us staring at a page
compression visits those readiest to evolve and will stress distances past due

we hold the unaccountable bodies we can't see as continuations of enigma
fused gargantuans beyond screens we can only imagine by the realms we attract

as we enter the edges ahead we listen with eyes not ears whole bodies left dormant
to attract the realms we need by making space for realms in need

            and now, something about the speed
        from ear to eye — so that *reading* attracts
                the *lived-hearing* we are
            to question — *what is lived* —

        did we never hear, with every part of us — so that
                people-staring
while staring back — calls out the part of us
            that reads us, while reading back

<< to be read — by what reads us — is a lived-reading >>

and now, a movement
trying to be heard — what part of us
is engaged
with our own impossibility, when we sit, to watch
— with ears

this intricate enclosure
<< definition as reality >>
is a gif I was born with *<< note missing "t" >>*

the word I am — is the word I read
<< and I can't read the human
if I can't be the human >>

evolution forces new speeds, for movement
we develop new organs to function
we are impossible question marks, curved
by human vocabulary — what face is yours
cured by vocabulary — by new limbs in movement

bird, I see you
but you saw me first
did we catch away
or look away, at the same time

[the interrupted blanket]

the effort to remain ambiguous
while your heart is beating
    — broken heart as shadowplay —

  I stand on the calculated cliff
inner rinsing against telestration
    — adhesion of a sun cloud —

  jagged reminders
trying to look past deeply torn tensions
    — just say it, are you fitting in or not —

  say *oh*, and make a *good* void
oh   how did that feel
    — what creates your properly responsive emptiness —

  where does my blinking mechanism
ride me, did you know
    — bees sleep in flowers holding each other's feet —

  and the unsleeping puzzle
    dreams
    — of its missing piece —

  the world outside these walls
is intent
    — on making me face it —

  am I to give in, or is that *giving in*
one kind of freedom
    — looking to fit in —

in particular lifetimes formed
of repetition is where cell di-
vision empathizes world divi-
sion, satisfying a temporary
reversal of body with light

is that interplanetary or just
in my head as a selving of
different worlds, sun travels
across my desk in reticulate
compartments, need to pull
the shades up, get something
to eat besides what I spill,
have to get more staying pow-
er into my sieve

the animals have our songs,
who we are, to infiltrate, what
we send, with removal, of all
we send, of what is

[textbook pacifist]

to inject *threat* into *thrive* — to fuse
terror into *tribe*, try explaining *surrender* as *survive*
or *fear* — as — *alive*
try accepting the collection of — *who you talkin' to*
as — an opacity of letters

that define the history of change
as *people* — or — *living scars in the form of*
animals who write — you know, the ones who attempt
infrastructure re-constructs that *beyond* the output of *misplaced spellings*
by *purposely* confusing the *reach* of — *what you just said*

to spell out — *achievement* — before — *wonder*
try spelling out the thought of *idea*
using the *of* that spells *connect* ——————┐
to *word* in the time of *body*
to the *already gone* of *this* body

> < THE WORD *OF* —
> THE DEFINITION *OF*
> — THE MAKING *OF* >

that makes — what I *don't* need to see
remind me — of what I *do* need to see
so I can say — what I *don't* need to say —
and be the *change* before the *get* —
dive into the cortex of a nation

incise *decision* out of skin — out of semen
out of blood — raise a question with an *image* — before a *thought*
compare *body* — to — *idea* < *being object that dies* >
to — *image* < *being thought that arouses idea*
with fight or flight >

escape or *be*
explain yourself — *inside* yourself
        inside your *making* — the age of talk
relies on speech — that doesn't
        explain but *looks*

        like you — *moving* on the inside
striving for transparent definition
        before finding who could be — *unknown*
unchanged — you know —
        someone like you

[into the enter]

To the rip at the end of the tapestry
   kRî kRî kRî
To the gigabyte Icarus fantasy
   wKî wKî wKî
To the sonic harmonic astronomy
   Naké Naké Naké
To the emerald light of ecology
   taKa taKa taKa
To the weapon you bait for the tyranny
   Kava Mavé Mava
To the hunger you keep for the colony
   Aba Cabu / Saba Cabé
To the hatch of obedient crackeries
   oBo oBo oBo
To the might of impossible mira-clés
   Eva Quaté-Quatoh

To the fissure's original fracture
Vvvv Vvvv Vvvv
To the fracture's original tremor
Wrrrr Wrrrr Wrrrr
To the tremor's original cry
Xocht Xocht Xocht
To sever the visible sky
Zrrrrrrrrrrrrrrrrrr to the shadow / undone
by the master / of none
                              therunner therunner / therun
therun
                    thescissor thepaper / thepebble therebel
                        thescissor thepaper / thepebble
therebel

                    the one / in guise of the other
                        in guise of the one / inside of the
other
                    the one / in guise of the other
                        in guise of the one / inside of the
other

                    themother thefather / theone theone
                        la lunala solala / luya
                    themother thefather / theone theone
                        la lunala solala / luya
To the infinite orbit of language
Gua Gua Gua
To the primal ascension of love
Qua Qua Qua
                        to the river / I river impossible
                    to the mountain / I mountain my name
                        to the fire / I fire ascension
                    to the enter / I enter my frame

to thebody thebody / thebrain thebrain
thespirit thespirit / thesame thesame
samesame / samesame
samesame / same
Seva sa / *Va*
Queva qua / *Va*
Weva ma / *Vaba va*
Leva ta / *Vaba ta*
Lenga ba / *Cumba ca*
Quay

themother thefather / theone theone
thescissor thepaper / thepebble
therebel

themother thefather / theone theone
thescissor thepaper / thepebble
therebel

themother thefather / theone theone
thescissor thepaper / thepebble
therebel

themother thefather / theone theone
thescissor thepaper / thepebble
therebel
— the invincible voice of humanity
Tzcha! Tzcha! Tzcha!
To the invincible voice of humanity
Tzcha! Tzcha! Tzcha!
To the invincible voice of humanity
Tzcha! Tzcha! Tzcha!
To the infinite orbit of love

we find ways to isolate truth
to isolate power
by calling on the shapes that save us
the shapes that survive us
out of brain
into body
we call on our instincts
to isolate hurt
away from emotion
to protect our power
we call on our truth
to attempt deflection
out of heart
we call on our hurt
to isolate deflection
away from the shapes that save us
the ones that define us
are the ones we call on
to survive our truth
our hurt
we call on our finding
out of knowing
away from doing
we find ways
to isolate truth

to sleep in anxiety
we find ways to dream of anxiety while sleeping through it
to dream of the relentless pounding of anxiety
we find ways to earnestly declare anxiety as a replacement for sleep
to darken a room by sleeping in it
we find ways to achieve darkness
to close our eyes in a darkened anxiety
to be reminded of anxiety during sleep
to achieve a darkened anxiety while closing our eyes in the being of anxiety

we find ways to know that we are sleeping
      to sleep in the knowing while describing to a lesser being the being of darkness
      to the being of a room lessened by becoming darkness
      to the lesser being lessened by being
      to assume hierarchy by states of being
we find ways to achieve status by stating anxiety in the realm of sleepless darkness
      to sleep in a darkened knowing of a lesser darkness
      to know there is another darkness
      to drop one for the other
      to one being the other's opening
      to encompass the lessons of concentration as a guise for meditation
      to spell differently the idea of quiet using meditation as a lark
      to leave this
      to become the one reading this instead of the one sleeping
we find ways

> *what is there to remember*
> *waiting deep in the folds*
> *of pixelated grey matter*
> *what lies beyond the new day*
> *an alarm that doesn't want to sleep*
> *in my house steady as a breeze*
> *a sound on a waking world*
> *unready for change the orange sun*
> *falls through my pockets and I think*
> *it's not me it's the world*
> *unrest at an easy juncture I step*
> *on a long night and nowhere*
> *was there a manual for keeping sane*
> *in the middle of the street heart sterilized*
> *in the back of a throat what is there*
> *to remember*

[of what is]

if I have mirrors of silence —
— parallels of silence — drawn, as if
it is only in breath
that path is *allowed* its breath
— as parallel to mine

if I am of mistakes, formed of mistakes —
— mistakenly informed of *night*
of its obligation for mystery —
— of *mystery* to mistake its night
informed by obligation

it is only — if *only* could be I —
that I grew up hearing, such tales
of hearing — so as to define *tales* — the idea
of tales, as accumulations of *hearing*
whispered into glass —
— the idea of glass, of what I can't touch
the idea of what I can't touch
— whispered into glass

if — as you say —
you have saying said to you — and I
have retreated into *self* as *path*
— as you say, longing for direction
back to a *self* being its retreat
as a substitute for *saying*, for lower-leveled *selfing* —
— for collecting tolls from severed sensitivities
from severed self
— from the severed self as a sensitive being
retreated

as if *reason* were enough for *ideals*, for empathetic
ideals — raised on severed selves,
once taught to retreat from what can't be touched —
— to *can't* once *reason* touched *ideal* — as if
it is, as you say, reason enough
for me to stop speaking —
— to start again when the *start again* stops,
you see

as if seeing were said in place of self —
— when saying *something*
— when *something* says I
— when I have *something* to say
retreat, let me, into my *saying* —
when I retreat *into* the saying of what I have,
— if I have taken on, as you say, the name of affluence
with generic tones
implicit generational tones influenced — by seers
of hierarchy — as practiced by non-colored room dwellers
Dwellers Of Room
the D.O.R.
by Dwellers Of Color
the D.O.C.

the modern D.O.C.
the D.O.C. of the *here*
this room right here, right now
you Dwellers
uncolored unbound by *now*
you Dwellers of Now
the D.O.Now
as if *how* were replaced by *saying*
as if *now* were replaced by saying D.
before O. or C. or Now

to give me *strange* for *strange* to be
to give me *off* for *off* to be
the D.O.C. of extraneous offerings
the Dwellers Of Offerings
the D.O.O. that *doo*
as if silence were beneath offering
as if silence were offering something, anything…
beneath voice

under the voiced a'neathing
voicing the 'neath
of 'neath as a form of *telling*
a form of saying what you say — by pulling in direction
what *away* wants to be
to you

what does *away* mean to you when you pull it
away from you
what does *away* tell you —
your voice — tell you
when pulled away from its its its
double my voice until I make *nothing* nothing underneath *'neath*
until I make nothing of your hearing
double my effect for gang-speak of *gangen-trecht*
milf und giver, fonged in'fleck
trice to say it, trice to say
try try try
how hearing you belongs to me
how *myst'er'y*
— into the taken drawn inspect
— into the only drawn wall I've seen as if
— drawing in your *(inhale…exhale)*

as if drawing walls into a room would inspect its generosity
its allowance of generosity
a parallel generosity
to you, right here, right now as if

the Generosity Offering Dwellers, you know
the G.O.D. be silent parallels of death of breath
if I as you have spoken clear
to what's in here —
— to what accumulates
to what in hear —
— to what informs in sight my sight
the token parallel
the stolen rear
the spice too hot
the exotic out licked one night
the one time just, one more — *right*
the sunken sail *past* right
the Dwellers drawn by para-might
by parasite
by light of likely window seen

to see
it is of seen
of what it is
to see

branched off by whatsoul

seedsorig

the fractured recovery

Indigo'rious

boho'genous

this vessel

mi todo

su todo

[junta]

what is the outshine — to step back into watching << *for volume*
       to take shape >> as i attempt
             to hold onto allowable tail
         << *to touch — everything i come in contact with* >>

to dismember *thought*   into avant sibling *sense*
        shaping << *deconstructed skat'po* >> with spillage
             << *an allowable act of misdeeds*
      given to those willing to disappear for a bit >>

if *mindself* serves *bodyself* — where to make room for *wordself*
        tongue << *direct organ to heart* >> << *what speaks of heart* >>
     takes root in heart — can *page* assume *body* for *breath*
      to slip through poem — between inked letters, is that symphony

      to *juxta-proposed* content, so this is — style
next phase — stuff   << *where tangent travels tendril* >> listen
        to stereo reception received   by the one ear
    << *i've lost track of the ins i'm out of* >> the modulation of completion

h/a/unted by the missing ear   enervate the composition — telegraphed
        by weight << *once lifted* >>   what is the work
      — to tolerate the intact   to take everything
            as everything << *to join in* >> to include

[dome]

flirting on a dome the pixie dust canary << *in plumed incantation* >>
     sends incomplete delusions for a desultory synopsis — with hunkered crest
     in hand   << *heft held by ankle lingam* >>

              — salivariate connoter
          talks   of editing as << *reinvention* >>
              of filtering as << *natural selection* >>
              re-named as << *separation* >>

<< *divergence* >> of our chosen consequence — the lone shift << *among these pages* >>
              to adapt — as << *nation* >> — am I
              of separation << *the question appears* >>
              — of zombie dust quixotic

phantom quiver quakes fluorescent sinner
        with reappearing scream << *immortal scar from my hand* >>

     — from gate   to lion   — *where best*

        to stretch out for reception — says message
     — *for clearest signal undercover of sleight* — says message
          — *to own the unformed* — says message

      << *to mine for things that don't mind things — know*
                   — what I mean >>

if *thing* were all there was — *skin* would let air in
but there
                  straddled on its back
       by open fate   is late arrival
             too wise   for action endearment

telegraci

      rewired as illusion

in recollect — of choosing

the sacral noose — is loosened

— now

dirty up

an' drop'em

— now slop

a drop

an'

now —

… lost it   damn …   *push …*   *push …*

on its way …   through *push*

o   o   o

— is *flow*   my life-affecting organism

rendered — as *push*

my inspiration to *day* through — with words

seeking — along its way

every other *push* to barrel through << *barrel through your push*

and you will demand your time, de-man your time >>

how to own your *push* — invoke the structure of your *flow*

tremble your vented oracle

re'orb the sun at the core of your back

<< *the day has found your split* >>

your drop — intense

and light — and how does that feel, compared

to when you started << *again, I talk, to no one there* >>

as nib goes dry — a slip

from hand, a longer dip

about to start — pen to page — the exact moment
of curve and stroke
revealed — taking a morning, to wander a morning

<< *I was so tired this morning*
and here I am, awake >>

at the jawbone edge of carrion encourager
unsettled on deciphering my body as Lucifer's timepiece
<< *the form I accept in the time of its motion* >>
my motion, my *it* map — the corners of my walk, previous and tense

<< *before dome slayed spirit out of form* >>
what do I call *spirit* — like essence, like seed
like demon gentility, far
from home

— but the *seeming edge* is what you reach
when trying to run, from
what you know — these words
how will they affect, what you know

<< *you right there*
me right here >> that porous engagement we breathe in
our desperation for alignment — in our time, in our spine
whose hands *are* these —

scarlessly writ like vapor   — *how many moves do I have left* —
transcending throat   — *is there a secret you could lift from me* —
blooded apparition   — *if words could come easy* —
disembodied enabler   — *just give in* —   to who
my edges
sudden, and all I own …

o o o

… what happened to my indents

the jumps
— from *margin*   — from *garden spot* to *flutter*   from *chyrsalis* —
                                                                to *flight* — my inside flight
                                                                — far from home

formless blinding light over me — finds a spot —
                — *give in* —   I hear, pressed underskin
                                   as knuckles reach solar plexus

            the word *eloquent*
            impaled
            on *din*   neurons numb divinity
                              << *what does the unknown need from me* >>

                from newly-edged limbs, as fingers reach
            the form I leave — impressions of solar organs
                continue sub-whispering their burn — that bruise

                where *no* feels safe
                where *don't* says *sure*...   I'll visit you
                                                    will you stay where you are?
                                                    take the limit I pour
                                                    as purity? — << *I hear myself*
                              re-hear my limits — as purity

                repeating a line — to hear it breathe
                              by saying it, repeatedly >> oh look

                                o o o

        m e m e   o n   m i s t   — *where are you going* ... I think, not write —
                                               letting third-eye return to maker

        p o e m   o n   m i s t   — *what are you giving* ... I think, not write —

takes serious length
        to make lift
      between the meridians
          — where the fault lines quake —

dig — into your *ment*
mo-*ment*
make-*ment*
state-*ment*
say-*ment*

in-*vent* oracle — offering intertwining tongues
            << *Rotorra … Musurra* >> — drop
             down to Sanskrit inertia

where chakras train the mindful
      stain the mind — both palms down
        for the *inner ride*
    the game of *un*
        done, as in, *I've been …*

                o o o

born twice because
of you — both low and through
our bloodlines
peaked in miscalculation, go ahead — fixate on my discoloration — see me
in you
           our lifetimes are so brief
             a work-in-progress

      scant unknowns, our needs
        undone — the making of our ideas
          the material possessions
    incinerating the lovely things
        the headless openings — vividly self-selecting …

— << I hear you talking

— do you hear me listening   *— sun >>*

o o o

— again, to you
I run —
pull me through
your blinding *new*

— the one
you slip behind, scattered
findings
lead me, off course — *solocoptro*

— I have
no one —
outside your whirling
rotro —

— what *eye* you
choose to enter
— which *eye* you
choose to own

— to elevate
illusion steal intention
from your home
— *day* —

— elemental slayer —
didn't I leave you
'fore the morn
— strung

by dawn — by temptation
centrifuged
at birth — each second
reverbed in sigma, sleighted sail

of scorch — of burn — of seek
sun — back to you
I come
— how is it —

when you —
— go low
is when —
you show your *most* you

or is that *new* you,
when you arrive — I go —
my rise —
our most *us* — the *deep*

I thought we were in
the lower we go — offered

∘ ∘ ∘

at the crux — where the hands find their *most* power
where the instrument lands, between the release of
invisible forces — exerted on structures
that affect circulation, structures that create compression
towards equilibrium, the same equilibrium
responding, to the compromise of circular growth — re-growing the cellular
to provide pores you were never ready for
to release the human capabilities, the barriers
preventing compassion — the compassion to transform
into a fully awake barrier, a sacral challenge —
to heal the alienation, we are born with — the one we are so good

at nurturing — to aspire dedication — towards true nature
      the pairing of our dual nature — accepting our greatest flow
between the polar opposites of our global intimacy — a sacred
      intimacy — acknowledging the value of contact
of rubbing up against skin — what invites the seen to the unseen
      the larger truth born of intimate contact — the greatest mystery
of life … that it's right there, underneath the skin — ready

        o o o

    the disappeared person — over there
    looking — through *their* world
    from *their* top — *here*
    but *not* — what
    is on your mind
    during rush hour
        — speed of night
        butterfly to fireflight
        lying in wait —
        beneath
        circulating appendix
        thorax of anxiety
        cantilevered crown —

    to *same* in the age of *talk*
    as *spirit* —
        to clean up
        a *now* — caught in the act
    the — *in* — of the effort involved
    — to — slow down

  << I choose to piss off the canon
        re-neg on all the good I done >>

— and there
just when *arrival*
— wrecked *asylum*
motion's apparition — declaws the invite

o   o   o

we move on, to the lost limbs
of us — our dots — connected
with loss, we break
        the luminous details — *does this hurt* —
                don't ask
                what you know the answer to

the apparition in question << *the open skull* >>
        does not answer your call, in chronological time
            — the obstacle
            that keeps you sustained
            by the thing you understand
            — *to wake you up, in your body* —

                                the last resistance I have
                                    is my body

        ageless — as we age
      the human spirit
        not physical, once born

o   o   o

the words have always been there — by moving the body
        through the body, byproducts of transition
        excrete into the system

let me open your episode
                              — the most visible poem says —
to work on your inflammatory response

        all tissues — open to the promise you put yourself in
        under someone's skin, realizing
                        the poem's spine
                        is the poet's

                        ○ ○ ○

        we stop a bit — to remember that taste of space
        from a few moments ago
                to unsettle the finished viewpoint
                — I think — the same person, yet limiting
                or being, the same

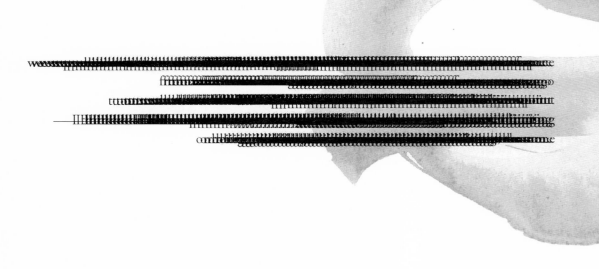

ifyouwannawatchyou
nosweat

nocareifyou
spiritonspire

likes
assownd

notstagebutspace
whereyou

worldisyoursalone
worldworldin

deeperthedemon
wouldletyou

what
do

atremorinthequa
thespaceyourein

youfind
whenalone

whereinthe
wouldyou

outsidenoself
actingas

canyounot
wouldyounot

noteventhere
thehigherhigh

thefeelingworld
ashauz

aspaceright
areif

howdoyoulet
soundsoundin

alignstheline
letworldin

would
that

atellerinthequa
thequa

yourselfwith
tono

whereyoulookinto
seeyourself

asthetremor
thequa

Edwin Torres is a poet, performer, sound visualist, graphic designer, and editor.
Previous books include: *The Animal's Perception of Earth* (DoubleCross Press),
Xoeteox: the infinite word object (Wave Books), *Ameriscopia* (University of Arizona Press),
Please (Faux Press cd-rom) and *Onamalingua: noise songs and poetry* (Rattapallax e-book).
He edited *The Body In Language: An Anthology* (Counterpath Press).
Edwin grew up in New York City.

ROOF BOOKS
the best in language since 1976

Recent & Selected Titles
- DEATH & DISASTER SERIES by Lonely Christopher, 192 p. $20
- THE COMBUSTION CYCLE by Will Alexander, 614 p. $25
- URBAN POETRY FROM CHINA: editors Huang Fan and James Sherry, translation editor Daniel Tay, 412 p. $25
- BIONIC COMMUNALITY by Brenda Iijima, 150 p. $20
- UNSOLVED MYSTERIES by Marie Buck, 96 p. $18.95
- MIRROR MAGIC by John Sakkis, 96 p. $18.95
- I AM, AM I TO TRUST THE JOY THAT JOY IS NO MORE OR LESS THERE NOW THAN BEFORE by Evan Kennedy, 82 p. $18.95
- THE COURSE by Ted Greenwald & Charles Bernstein, 250 p. $20
- PLAIN SIGHT by Steven Seidenberg, 216 p. $19.95
- IN A JANUARY WOULD by Lonely Christopher, 90 p. $17.95
- POST CLASSIC by erica kaufman, 96 p. $16.95
- JACK AND JILL IN TROY by Bob Perelman, 96 p. $16.95
- MOSTLY CLEARING by Michael Gottlieb, 112 p. $17.95
- THE RIOT GRRRL THING by Sara Larsen, 112 p. $16.95
- THOUGHT BALLOON by Kit Robinson, 104p. $16.95
- UN\ \MARTYRED: [SELF-]VANISHING PRESENCES IN VIETNAMESE POETRY by Nhã Thuyên, 174 p. $17.95
- ECHOLOCATION by Evelyn Reilly, 144 p. $17.95

Roof Books are published by Segue Foundation
300 Bowery • New York, NY 10012
For a complete list, please visit roofbooks.com

Roof Books are distributed by
SMALL PRESS DISTRIBUTION
1341 Seventh Street • Berkeley, CA. 94710-1403.
spdbooks.org